Pasadena Oaks

By Jennifer Bentson

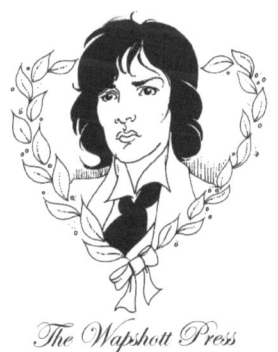

Pasadena Oaks
by Jennifer Bentson

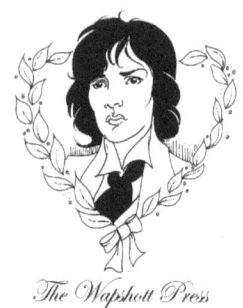

Published by
The Wapshott Press, LLC
PO Box 31513
Los Angeles, CA 90031
www.WapshottPress.com

Copyright © 2016 images by Jennifer Bentson
Copyright © 2016 collection Wapshott Press
Copyright © 2016 articles by respective authors

First printing June 2016

All rights reserved. No part of this is publication may be reproduced or transmitted in any form or by any means, electronic or mechanical, including photocopy, recording, or any information storage and retrieval system now known or to be invented, without permission in writing from the publisher, except by a reviewer who wishes to quote brief passages in connection with a review written for inclusion in a magazine, newspaper, or broadcast.

ISBN: 978-1-942007-06-7

06 05 04 03 4 3 2 1

Wapshott Press logo by Molly Kiely

Pasadena Oaks

Table of Contents

Preface
i

The Beginning
1

District One
3

District Two
7

District Three
9

District Four
13

District Five
23

District Six
29

District Seven
39

Oaks Outside of Pasadena
59

Caltech Tanka Tour
70

About Jennifer Bentson
75

ACKNOWLEDGEMENTS

The City of Pasadena has been a hub for the Oak Tree Community. The Pasadena Oak, also known as the Engelmann Oak is a somewhat rare oak that is well known in Pasadena. The City selected my proposal to create a book about the Oaks of Pasadena and I want to thank them deeply for this opportunity to do this project. My partners in the community have met my needs with enthusiasm and joy. I want to acknowledge the "village" it took to make this all possible.

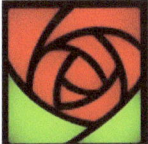 **PASADENA**

*Made possible in part by the Pasadena Arts & Culture Commission
and the City of Pasadena Cultural Affairs Division*

Mayor Terry Tornek
Councilmember, District 1, Tyron A.L. Hampto, Cushon Bell and Cheynne Chong
Councilmember, District 2, Margaret McAustin and Margo Morales
Councilmember, District 3, John J. Kennedy and Jana N. West
Councilmember, District 4, Gene Masuda and Noreen Sullivan (already in the book)
Councilmember, District 5, Victor M. Gordo and Vannia DeLaCuba
Councilmember, District 6, Steve Madison and Takako Suzuki
Councilmember, District 7, Andy Wilson and Pam Thyret

Grace Anderson, Typo Guru	Darya Barar
Helena Bowman, Botanist	Rochelle Branch, Arts and Culture, City of Pasadena
Nina Brey, World Famous Picture Framer	Emina Darakjy
Delmy Emerson, Caltech	Emily Hopkins, Sidestreet.org
Evan Jackson, Assistant	Alan Lamson
Annette Martinez, Cordon Bleu	Ginger Mayerson, Wapshott Press
Kirk Myers, Pasadena History Museum	Pasadena Conservancy of Music
Melissa Perez, Pasadena Main Library	Jan Pingleton
Dr. Kimberly Shugart	Nancy Stone
Palencia Turner	Sarah Weber
Teri Weeks	Kathabel Wilson, Caltech Poets On Site
Helen Wong, Eaton Canyon Nature Center	Allen Zorthian, Zorthian Ranch

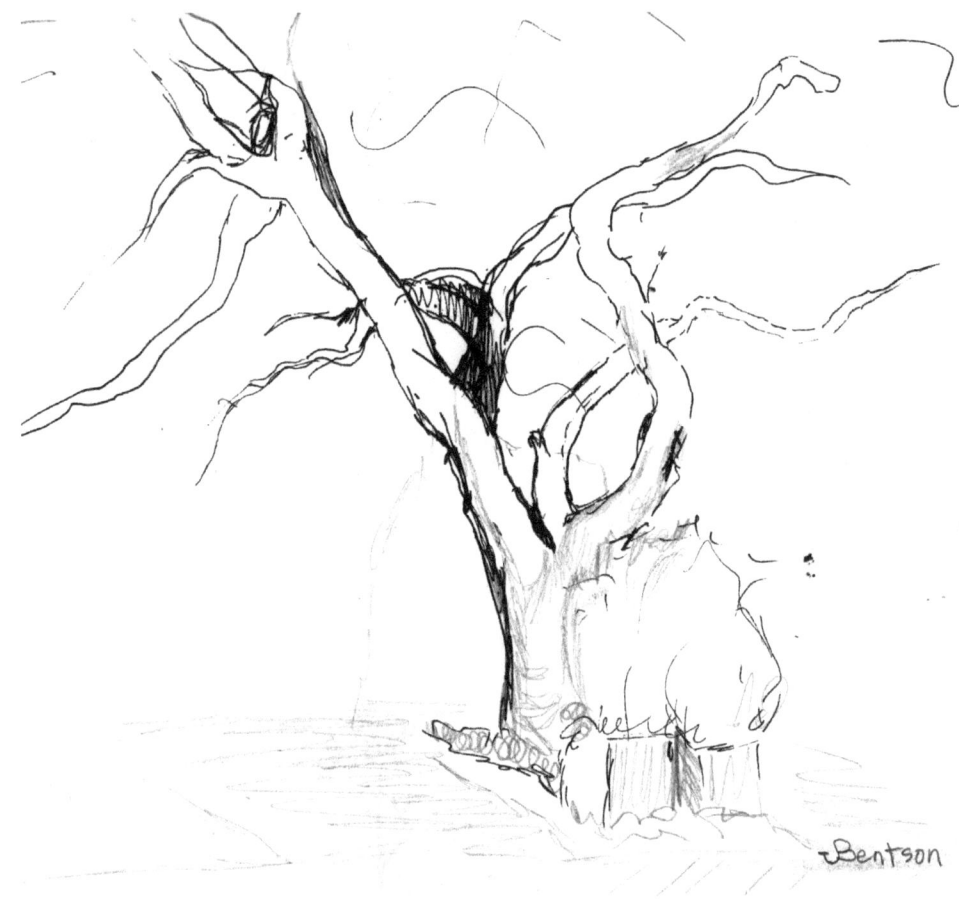

Charcoal Sketch of the Largest Engelmann Oak in the USA in Pasadena, CA
By Jennifer Bentson, Charcoal on Paper, 8.5" x 11"

PREFACE

I began painting oak trees at about the same time I started taking workshops in figure drawing. The two seemed to blend together in my mind as I walked through the local gardens and looked up at the Coastal Oak tree limbs. It was just that simple; limbs both human and oak were fascinating to me.

My soul desired purpose, and on the surface, painting the significant oaks in my community was a way to preserve them and celebrate them while they are alive.

As an artist who was locked inside of a business person for over 30 years, this was my journey to myself.

Pasadena Oaks

by Jennifer Bentson

THE BEGINNING

The first oak of my muse was in Descanso Gardens. I stretched out under the oak and looked skyward at the limbs crossing overhead. Then I returned later and the oak tree had been chopped down and mulch covered the place where that oak once lived.

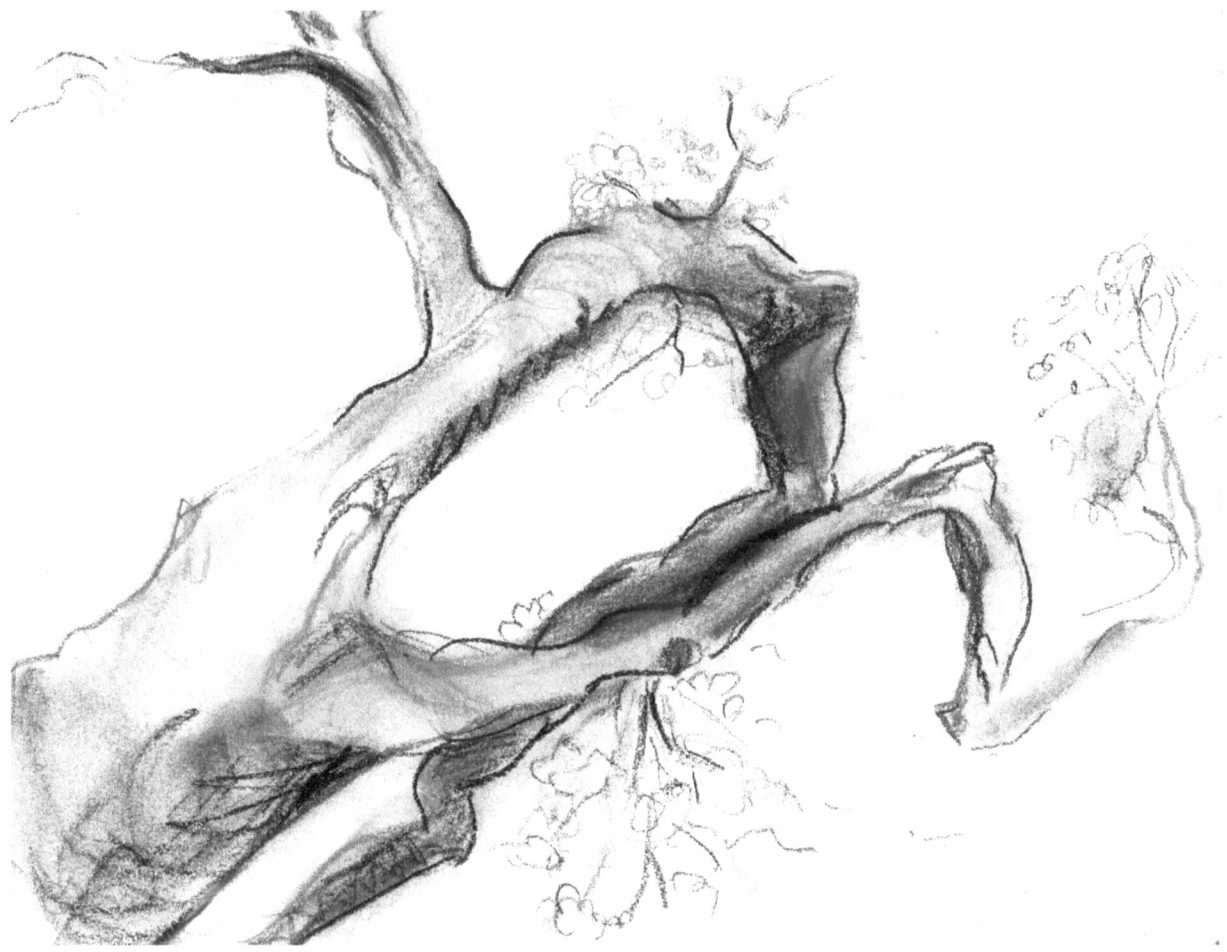

Oaks Looking Skyward, by Jennifer Bentson, 11" x 8.5", Charcoal Sketch
Sketched at Descanso Gardens

I felt like I had lost a friend. Losing that oak reminded me of the loss of my business by legislation, and in the same year the loss of my dear husband.

Life had taken a left turn for me. I was enveloped in sorrow and paperwork. The trees seemed to be so peaceful and undemanding.

Do I believe they have a spirit? Yes, and that spirit helped to heal me and allowed my artistic side to blossom and grow. My inner voice was saying how the oaks, common, yet unique have a voice and a story. Like a chorus we sing together and create something truly wondrous.

On a practical side, since I have started to paint oaks, we have lost many significant ones. They have been energetically thrown into the wood chipper and their images forgotten, let alone their stories. This book will tell some stories and show some images. Enjoy!

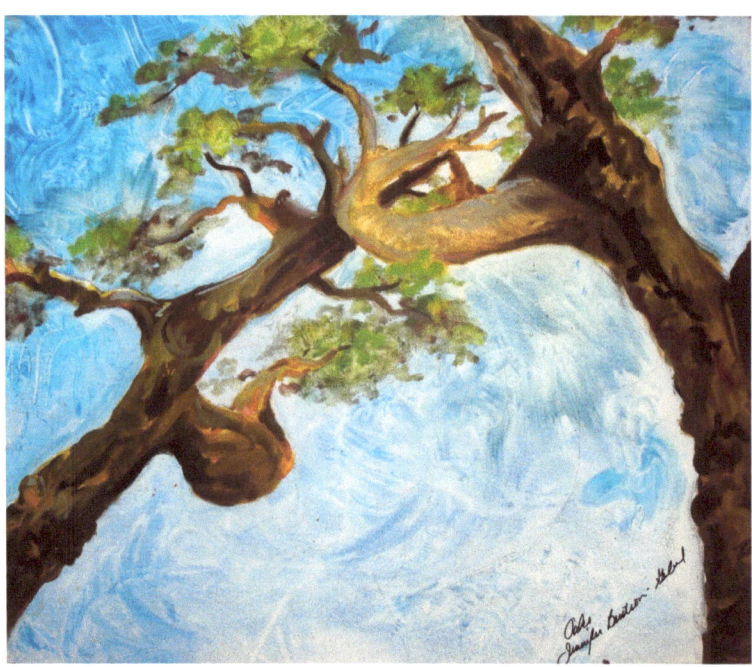

Oaks, by Jennifer Bentson-Gebel, 16" x 20", Oil on Canvas
First Oak Painting, Descanso Gardens

PASADENA COUNCIL DISTRICT ONE

The Arroyo Seco is a wonderful area in Pasadena that encompasses the Rose Bowl, Two Golf Courses, the Kidspace Children's Museum and the Aquatic Center where you can watch future Olympians practice diving. The Arroyo is also a canyon channeling water from the Angeles Forest into the LA River. Spanning the Arroyo are several bridges, but one stands out for it's tragic legacy. This bridge is known as the Colorado Bridge. It has been nicknamed "Suicide Bridge".

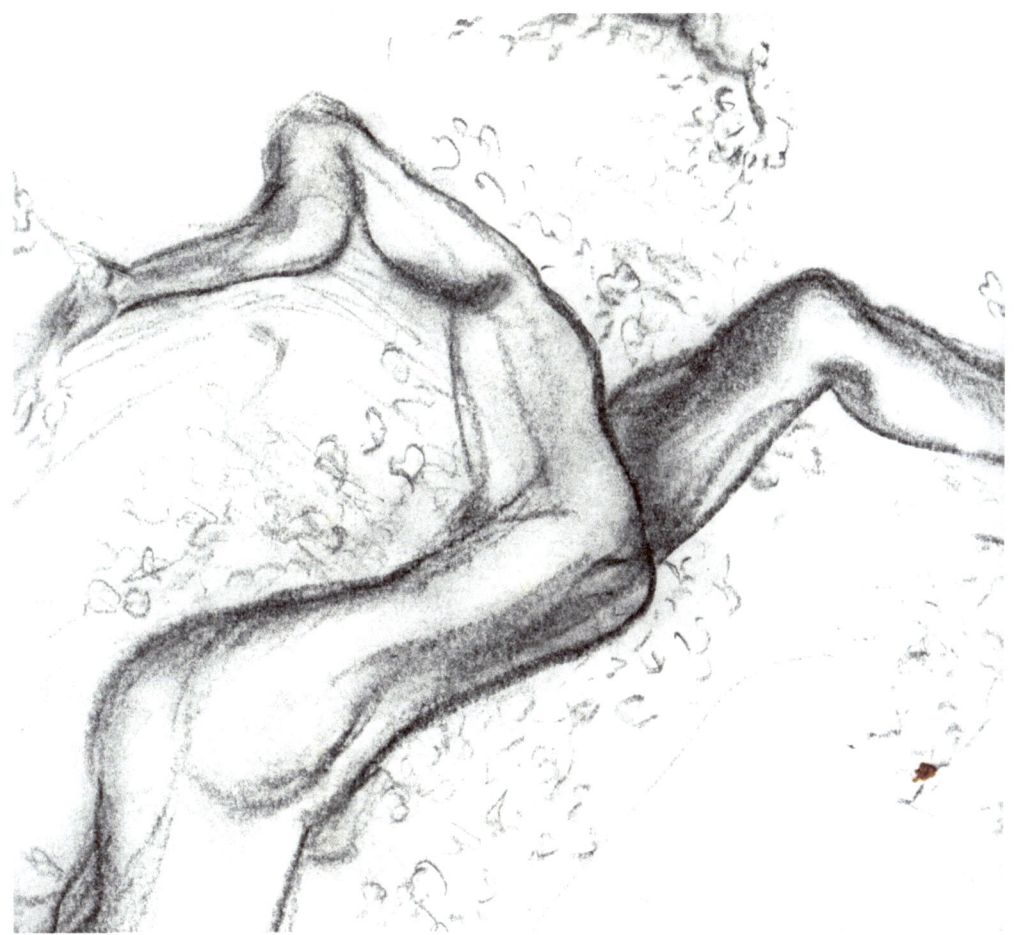

Limbs and Legs, by Jennifer Bentson, 11"x14", Charcoal Sketch
Sketched at Bottom of the Arroyo Seco

The story unfolds that during the construction of the bridge in 1913 a worker fell into the wet concrete and was left inside the bridge structure. Stories of deaths associated with this bridge have continued until today. It is recorded that there are over 100 deaths of people jumping from this bridge. Lots of artists capture this bridge in their paintings of the Arroyo. I painted this bridge from the viewpoint of an oak tree growing at the bottom of the Arroyo.

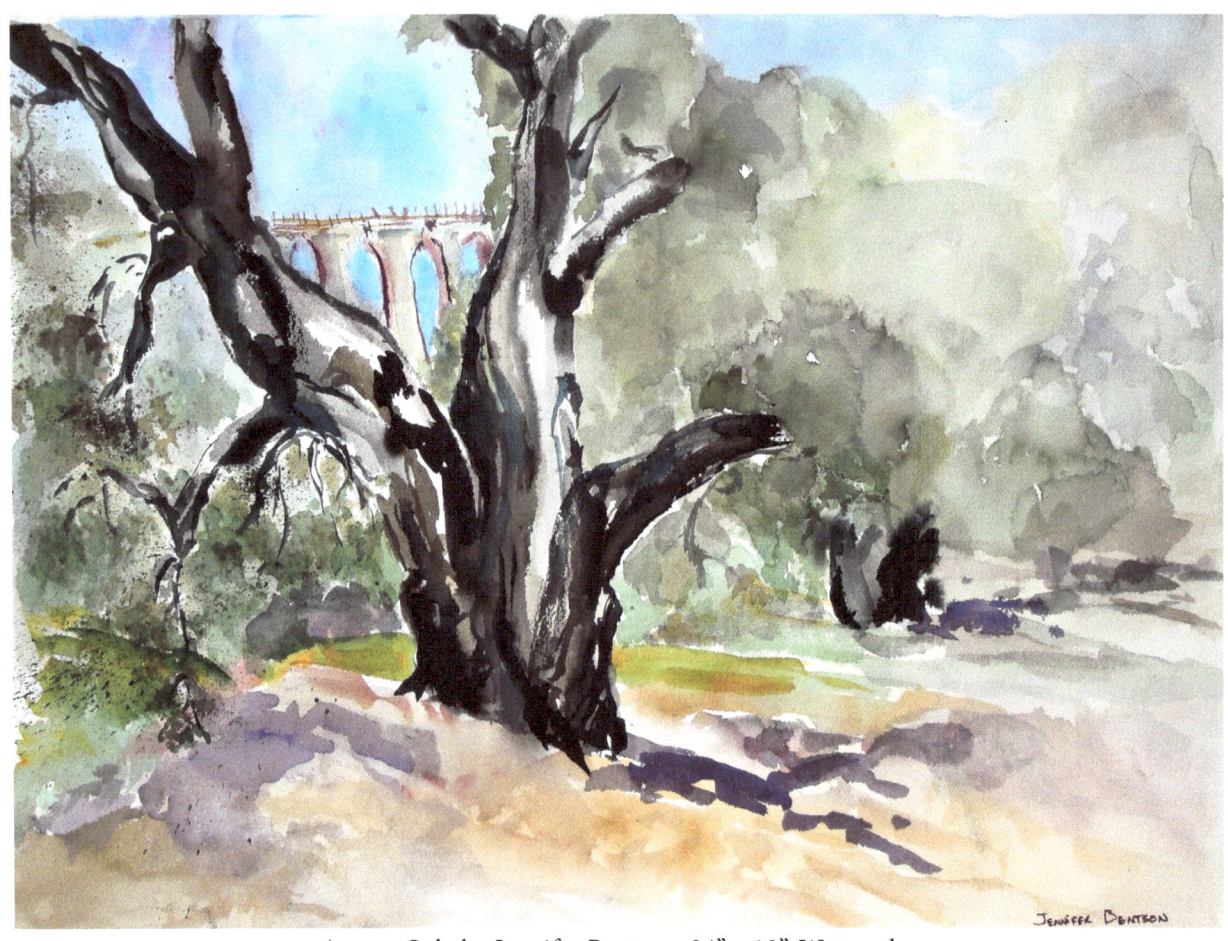

Arroyo Oak, by Jennifer Bentson, 24" x 18", Watercolor

Painted on location at the bottom of the Arroyo Seco looking up to Colorado Bridge

HAHAMONGNA OAKS

The Hahamongna Watershed is an important watershed for this area. It is where the mountain water runs off into the Devil's Gate Dam and eventually the LA River.

These oaks are from the park at the edge of the Devil's Gate Dam area. Hahamongna was a tribe of Tongva Indians. This is a beautiful area to have a picnic and enjoy the large oak trees. Jet Propulsion Laboratories is just up the street from this park.

I was in a car accident and had to have hip surgery. At the time I had a convertible car. So I put the top down and sat and painted this painting.

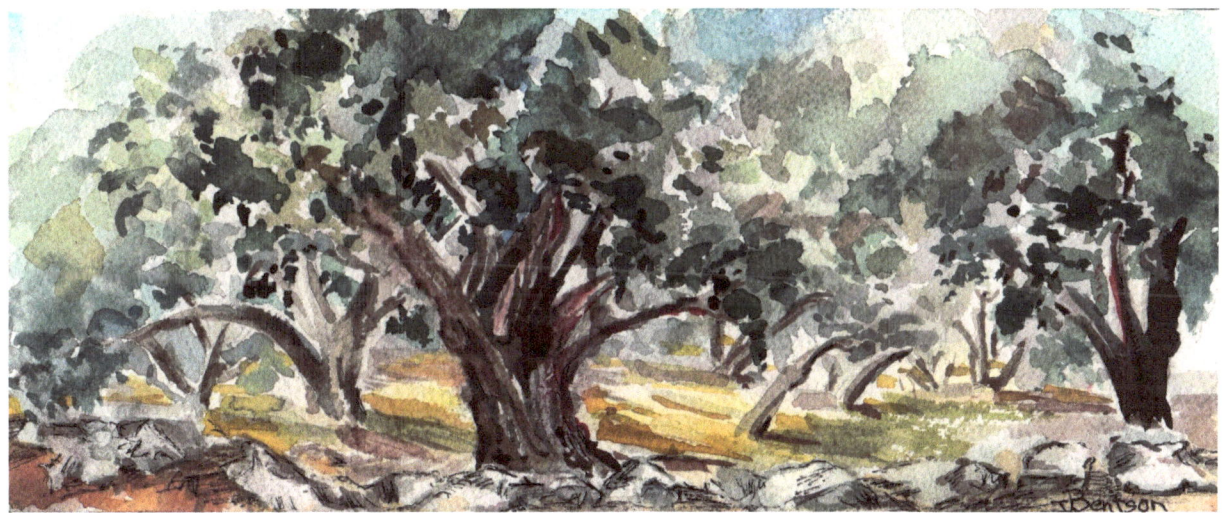

Hahamongna Oak Grove, by Jennifer Bentson, 9.25" x 3.5", Watercolor

Painted on location.

COUNCIL DISTRICT TWO

The Difference between two Common Oaks in Pasadena

In Pasadena, we commonly find two different oak trees: the Engelmann Oak (*Quercus engelmannii*) and Coast Live Oak (*Quercus agrifolia*). The Engelmann Oak goes by many names; Pasadena Oak, Heritage Oak or Mesa Oak. The Coast Live Oak and the Pasadena Oak are easily separated by their leaves, acorn, and stature.

The Engelmann Oak is the rarer of California oaks. It has a small distribution and the Pasadena area is its northern most natural outpost. From here it grows south towards Riverside, San Diego and Baja California. The Coast Live Oak is common in California. It grows up and down the state.

The Engelmann Oak grows straight, with a single trunk and an open crown. This gives it an airy and light stature. The leaves have a waxy coating which makes them appear greyish or silvery. The leaf margin is usually smooth (or slightly wavy), with no spines or hairs. The Engelmann acorns are short and stubby and on the small side. The little cap on the acorn is quite knobby. The tree bark is light, whitish to light gray. The older the tree, the more furrows the bark will have.

The Coast Live Oak is another oak you will find in Pasadena. It grows more as a dense dark green tree. The trunk(s) often leans sideway or looks a little off-balance. The leaves are convex (cup-shaped), shiny green with spines on the margins. Underneath they have brownish hairs, often most noticeable where the veins meet the midvein towards the leaf-stem (like a fuzzy armpit). The acorns are long and narrow with a tapered end. The acorn cap has scales that hug the fruit. The Coast Live Oak has smooth grey bark, but it furrows at it grows older.

Helena Bowman, Botanist

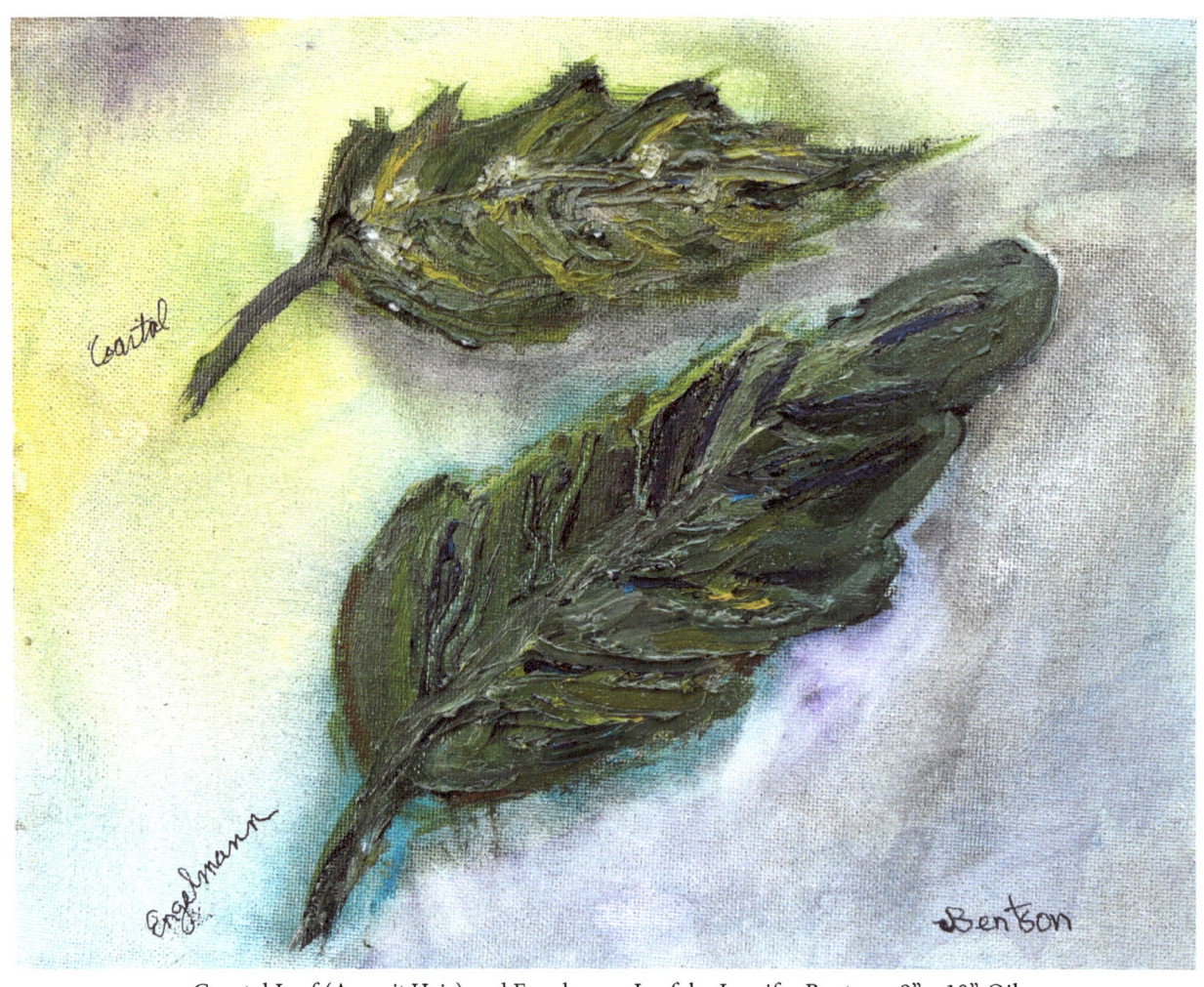

Coastal Leaf (Armpit Hair) and Engelmann Leaf, by Jennifer Bentson, 8" x 10", Oil

Painted in studio

COUNCIL DISTRICT THREE

The City of Pasadena has thousands of mature trees that contribute long-term aesthetic, environmental and economic benefits to the City. The City places great value on its trees, and in 2002 the City Council amended the Municipal Code to establish the City Trees and Tree Protection Ordinance (TPO). The goals and objectives provided in the TPO include growing Pasadena's canopy cover by increasing the protections for trees on public and private property. Through these protections, the City Council aspired to protect the visual and aesthetic character of the City, thereby enhancing the quality of life for residents, visitors and wildlife. Inherent in the value of the urban forest are resources that are often overlooked. Trees provide a habitat for wildlife, protection from climate variations, and trees serve as the thread that ties neighborhoods together.

Darya Barar, City of Pasadena Arborist

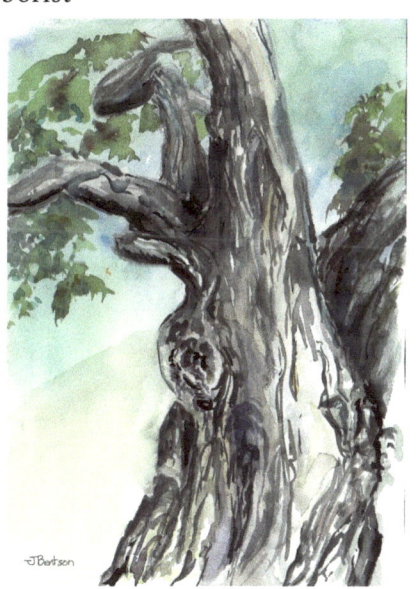

Jen's Oak, by Jennifer Bentson, 9" x 12", Watercolor

Painted in my backyard

Pasadena Beautiful has been an active organization in the advancement of the Engelmann Oak. Beautifying Pasadena and planting trees was the reason Pasadena Beautiful Foundation (PBF) was founded in 1960. One of the primary goals is to continue to purchase and plant trees around Pasadena when required. PBF has a 50-year history of working with the City of Pasadena to plant trees and protect our urban forest.

I learned about a reforestation project along Holly Avenue. Emina Darakjy told me that the Carob trees were in bad shape and the City of Pasadena removed them. The walkway was replanted with the Engelmann Oaks.

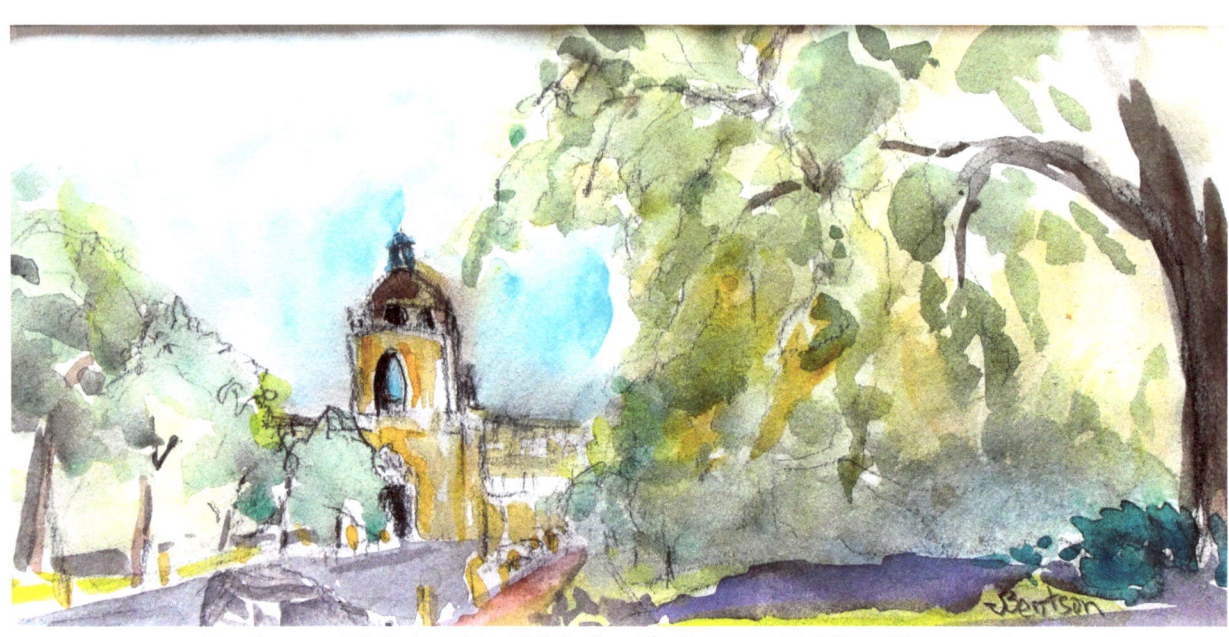

Engelmann Oak Path to City Hall, by Jennifer Bentson, 11.25" x 3.5", Watercolor

Painted in my studio from sketches by Jennifer Bentson

GHOST OAK OF MEMORIAL PARK

I first met with Darya Barar of the City of Pasadena to identify significant oak trees in 2011. I learned about the great oak in Memorial Park. In December of 2011 there was a tremendous wind storm. The oak at Memorial Park fell before I was able to paint it. Two days after it fell, I painted the oak. It was strewn over the sidewalk, park and street. It truly was a grand oak. I went on to paint many more oaks that Darya had told me about along with oaks identified by the various council districts.

Sadly, many oaks are leaving us. I hope this project helps to protect our oaks.

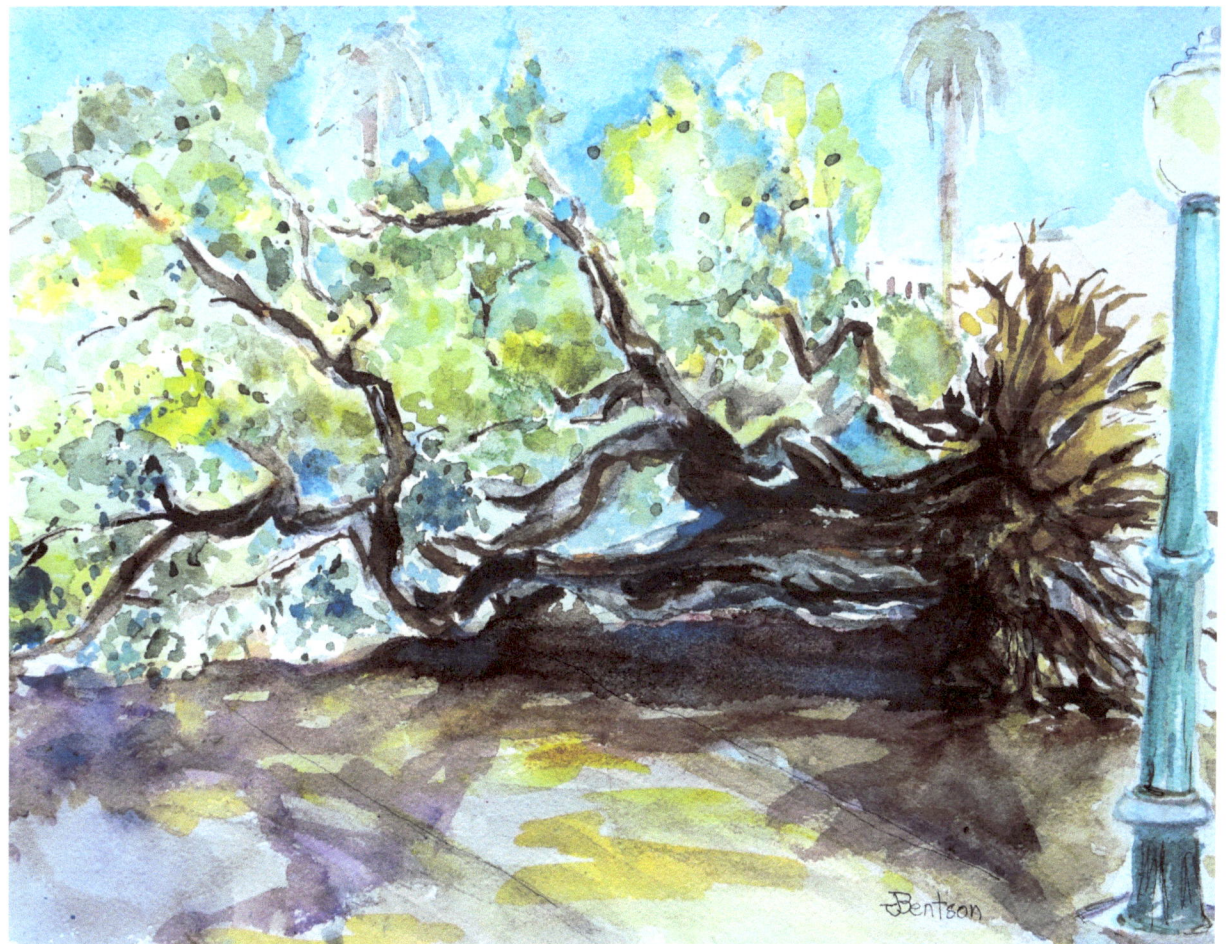

Ghost Oak Of Memorial Park, by Jennifer Bentson, 9.75" x 13.25", Watercolor

Painted on location.

COUNCIL DISTRICT FOUR

Councilmember Gene Masuda and his assistant, Noreen Sullivan sent out an email blast to interested community leaders. They asked for help with my project.

I received many responses and was so very glad to see the oaks of District 4.

District 4 is home to Eaton Canyon and abuts the San Gabriel Mountains.

Frank and Janis Crowhurst's Family Tree

by Nancy Crowhurst-Stone

Mom and Dad bought their perfect home in upper Hastings Ranch in 1958. They enjoyed the location of the house so close to nature and the mountains. At the edge of the property was a lovely oak tree which shaded my brother, Bill, my sister, Sue and me as we played in the backyard. Then, in 1961 there was a terrible fire that threatened the oak and the home. My father, Frank, stood on the roof of our home and fought the fire with his garden hose. He sprayed the oak, which was on fire and kept the roof and surrounding area wet. The Fire Department urged Frank to evacuate and let the fire take over. But my father was a fighter. He stayed and kept the water flowing. As a result only half of the oak tree burned. And, by some miracle, now over 50 years later that same oak has become the grand dame of the neighborhood. And now, my daughter, Sarah lives in this home with her family. Frank and Jan's great grandchildren play under this oak and enjoy the peace and shade of the oak which was saved over 50 years ago.

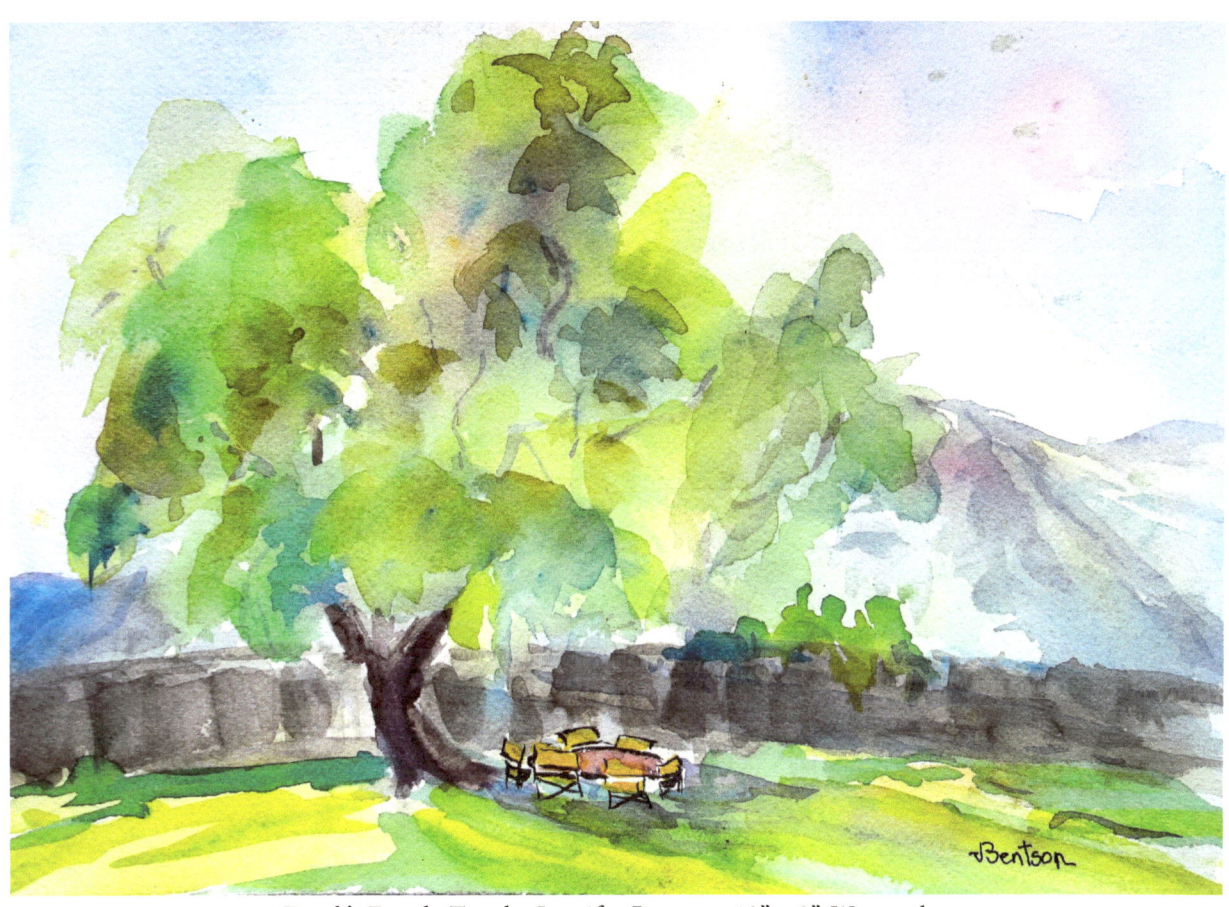

Frank's Family Tree by Jennifer Bentson, 12" x 9", Watercolor

I visited the tree and took many photos which were used in this painting.

EATON CANYON NATURE CENTER

My friend, Helena Bowman, a Botanist and an artist told me about the oaks of Eaton Canyon. Helen Wong, employed by the Nature Center met with me and told me the story of "Mama Oak".

Mama Oak is a large coastal oak that shades the picnic area by the Nature Center. Helen said it is known as Mama Oak or Grandma Oak because when you sit at the picnic tables the arms of the tree seem to hug you, like a mother.

This is where over 11,000 school children convene each year to learn about nature and the fauna and flora of Eaton Canyon. Most of them sit right there under Mama Oak while docents and naturalists enliven the Earth we live on through talks and walks.

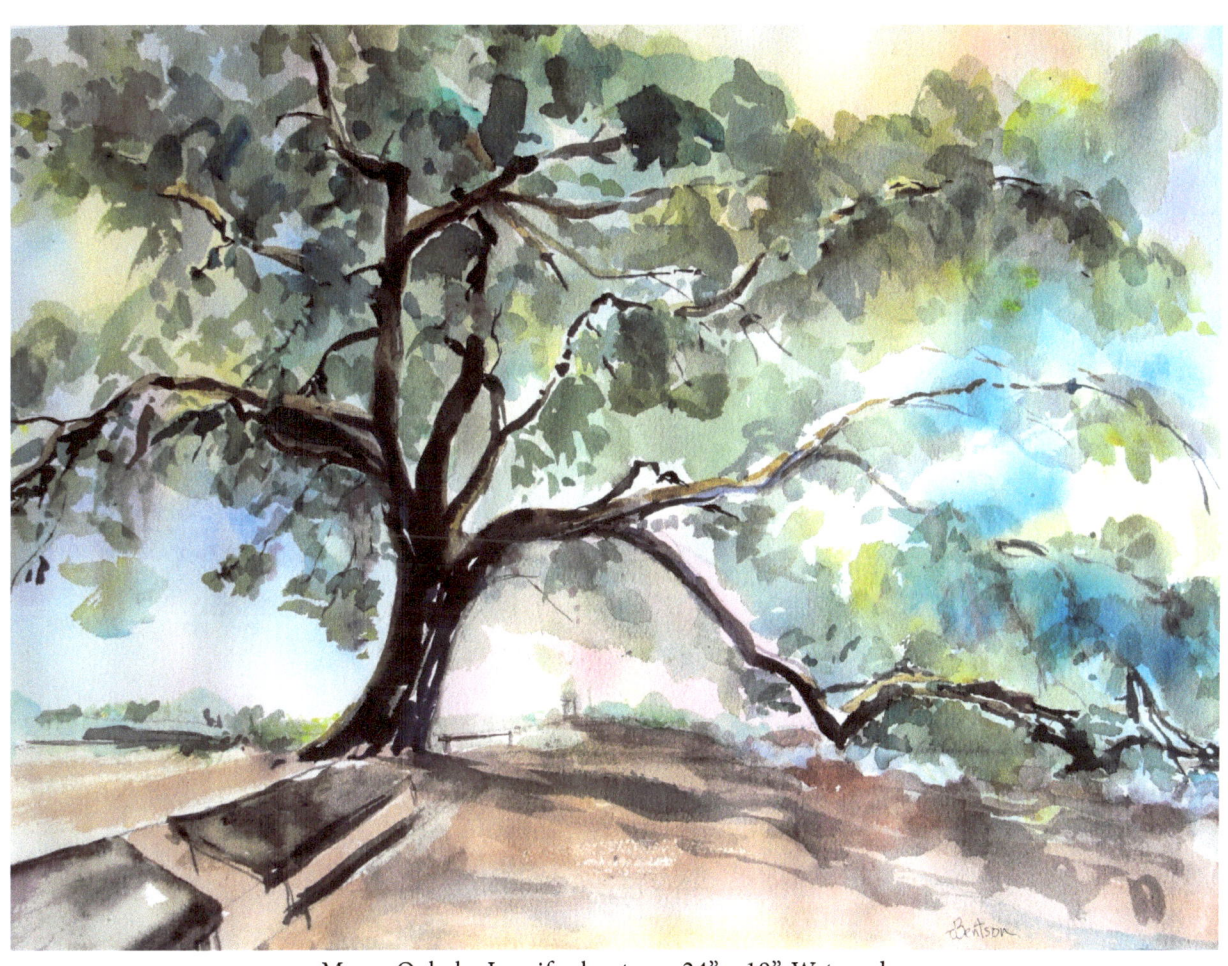

Mama Oak, by Jennifer bentson, 24" x 18", Watercolor

Painted on location at Eaton Canyon

PAINTING WITH A FRIEND

Helena Bowman is one of those friends who is always there for you. She is a happy and willing companion for painting, stuffing envelopes, or hanging an art show. And she is a botanist and artist. So she has been an enthusiastic partner in my Pasadena Oaks Project.

We both went to Eaton Canyon in search of the best oaks to paint. While we were there we tromped through the plants and Helena pointed out the nettles and poison oak. Good thing, because I would have come home to itchy memories of the day without her. She is a competent hiking partner.

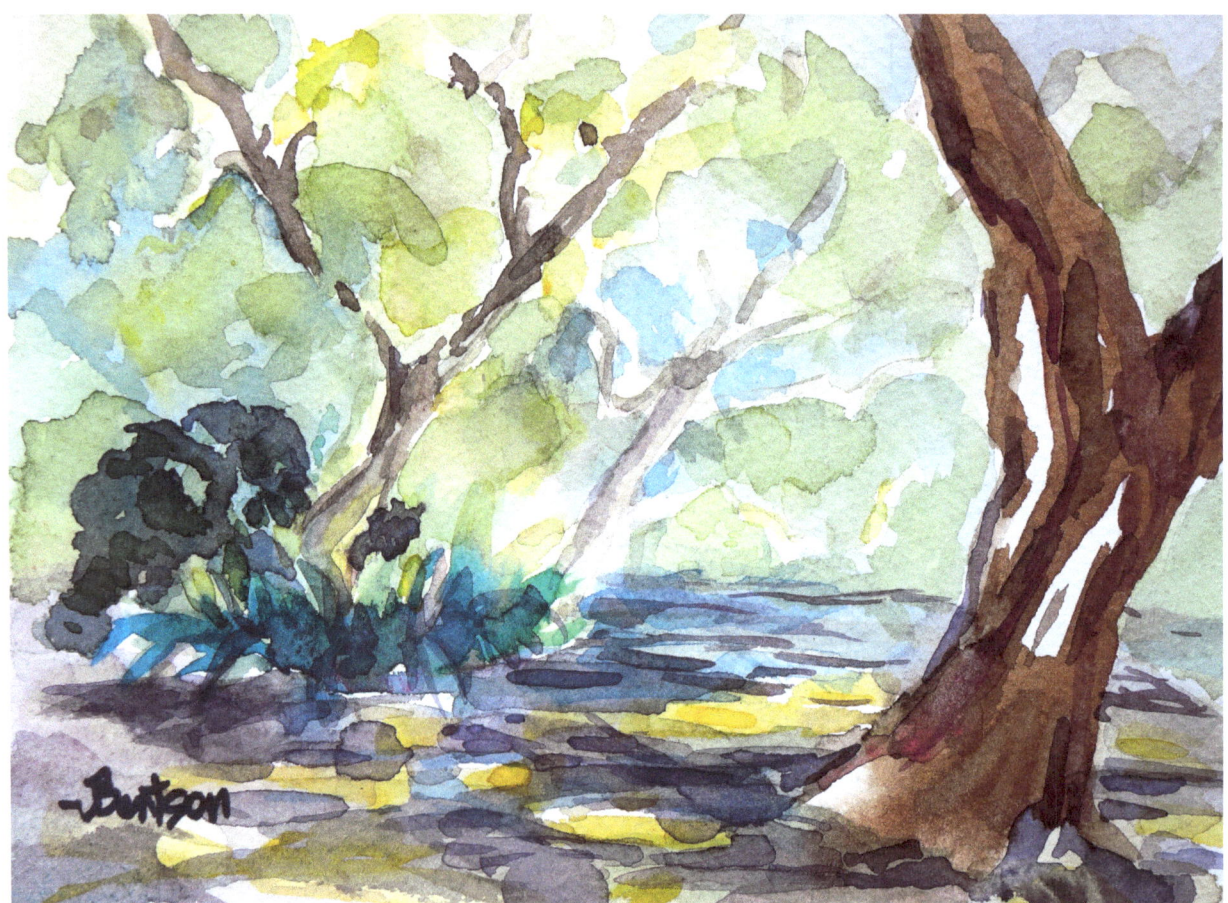

A walk in the Forest, by Jennifer Bentson, 6" x 4", Watercolor

Painted on location at Eaton Canyon

The Artist as a Writer/Poet

I have a cousin who once told me that its better to be very active in one or two groups than to join many. That is the thought that ran through my head when asked to be President of the San Fernando Valley Art Club. I said yes. And what a journey that turned out to be.

One adventure happened when I was at the front door greeting the members who came for our regular monthly meeting. The lady said her name was Lillian. I looked up and there stood my old high school English teacher. I asked if she ever taught English at my high school and she answered yes. I reminded her that she had been my English teacher. This was 40+ years ago.

Later, I received a phone call from Lillian. She said she had found a book of poetry I had written. Really? I didn't know I wrote poetry. We agreed to meet for lunch and Lillian produced a weathered green report folder with poetry. I recognized my handwriting and was astonished I had written 21 poems. I asked her why she had never given the assignment to write poetry back to me. She said she kept a few of the works of students she thought were outstanding. At the end of lunch, my 91-year old teacher asked me "So what ever happened to you?" The question hit me like a bell ringing in my ears. I took the poems, read them and thought to myself they were actually pretty good. I transcribed them. Lillian then called me and asked for the green weathered report book back. I gave it to her, but still have the poetry.

It was Lillian who inspired my writing at age 62. Because of her, I tried writing for an art magazine, Art Quench Magazine. The owner of the magazine is so supportive of my articles.

Finding my poetic self, I encountered a wonderful person who hosts a group of active poets at Caltech as well as in the area.

At the end of this book are poems from this group about the 400 plus year old Caltech Engelmann Oak from the Caltech Poets Club led by Kathabela Wilson.

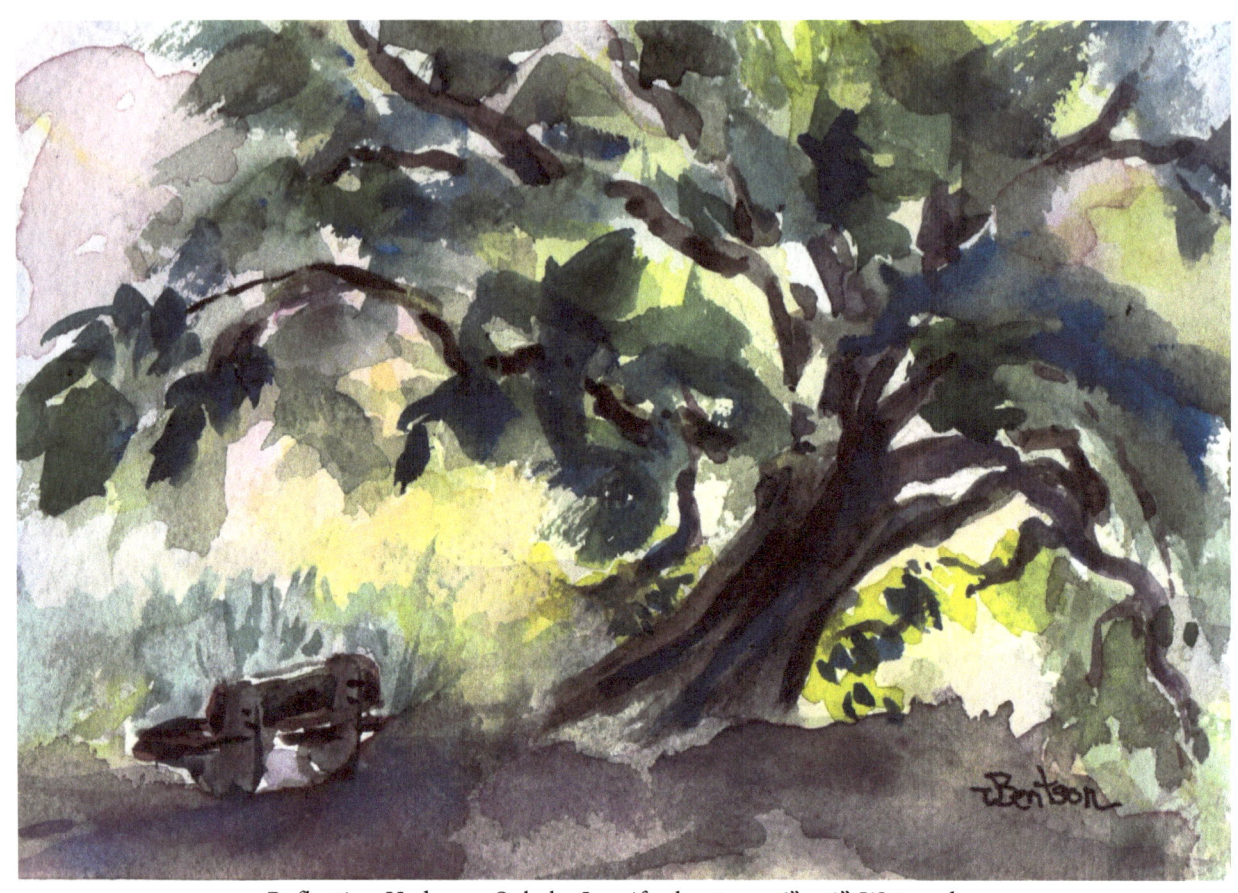

Reflecting Under an Oak, by Jennifer bentson, 6" x 4", Watercolor

This was painted at Eaton Canyon.

PALETTE KNIFE

This Painting was created using a palette knife.

Frankly, I had painted many paintings and there was a lot of smushed paint on my Pallette. So, rather than waste paint, I grabbed my palette knife and created this painting.

My father grew up in the Depression, and had what I call Depression-Era thinking. It is that type of thinking that sometimes sparks my creativity. Like this painting, I was too conservative to waste left over paint. I could hear my father's voice saying, there is a lot of paint there you could still use. So I scraped up the paint with a palette knife and created this.

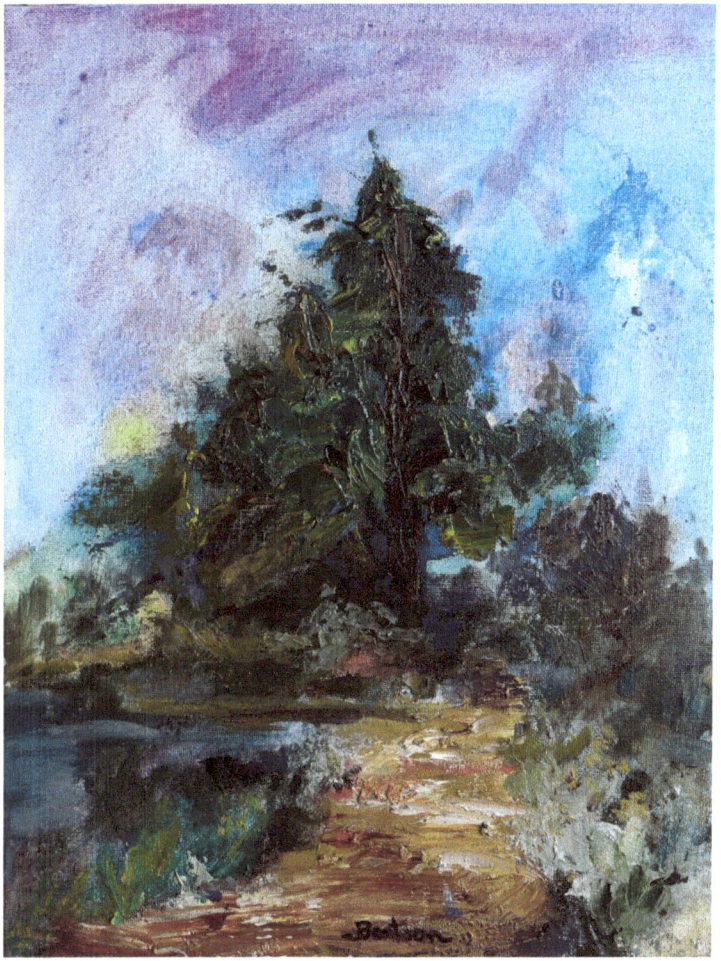

Eaton Canyon Path, by Jennifer Bentson, 11" x 14". Oil on Board

Painted in my kitchen

COUNCIL DISTRICT FIVE

The Oak That Helped Spread Art to Pasadena

Side Street Program (www.sidestreet.org) told me about a wonderful oak that shaded their mobile classroom/offices for seven years. It grew to be larger on one side than the other due to the care of the Executive Director, Emily Hopkins and her staff.

The Side Street Program offers art resources for the school classroom, active artists, and has a plethora of equipment for artists to use. We discussed the oak tree that shaded her project headquarters, two trailers, for seven years. Now, the oak shades the construction home for a Senior Apartment Project on Orange Grove and Fair Oaks Avenue. It is growing between Church's Chicken and the Senior Apartments on Fair Oaks and Orange Grove.

From Emily Hopkins, Executive Director

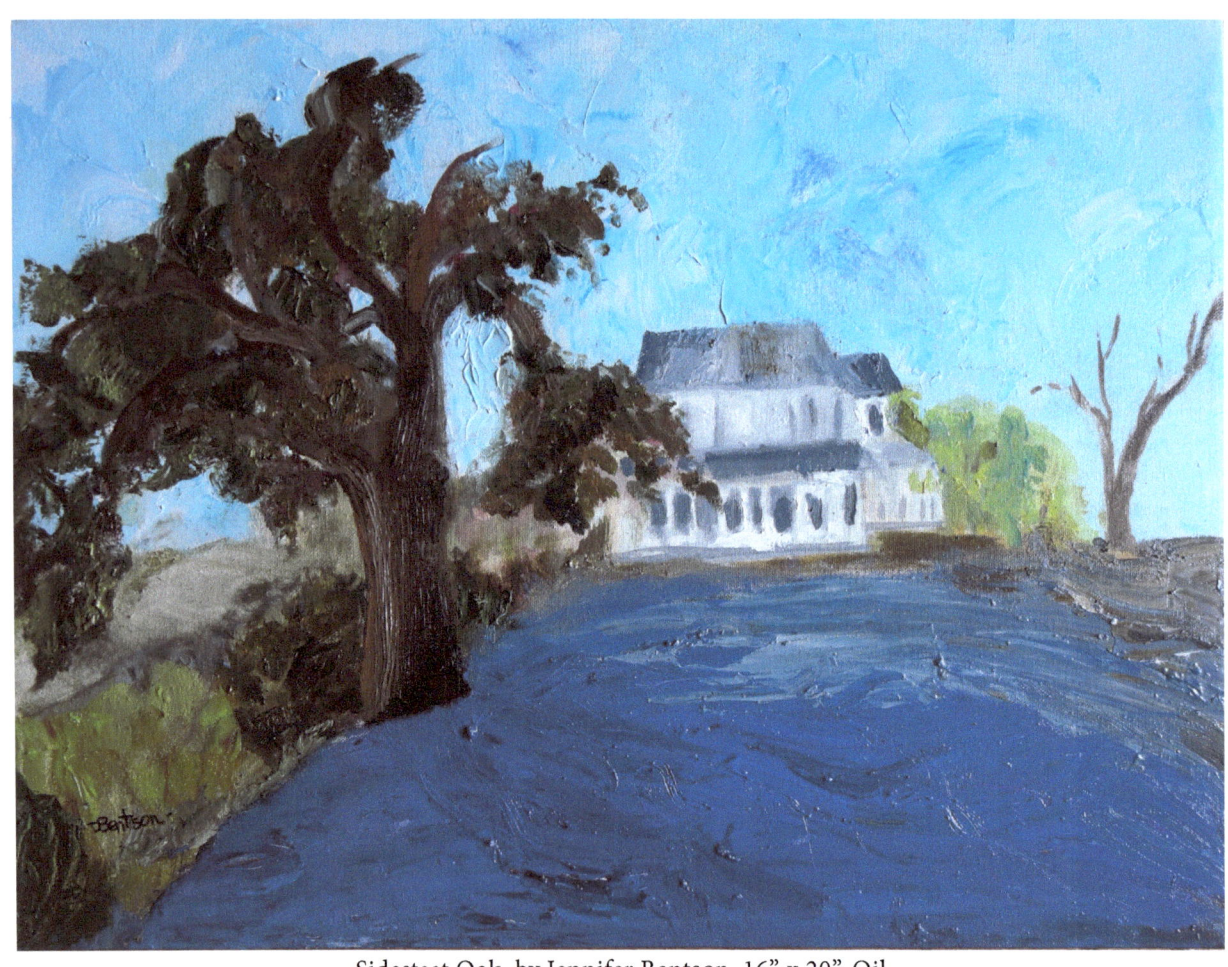

Sidesteet Oak, by Jennifer Bentson, 16" x 20", Oil

Painted in Studio

Side Street Program

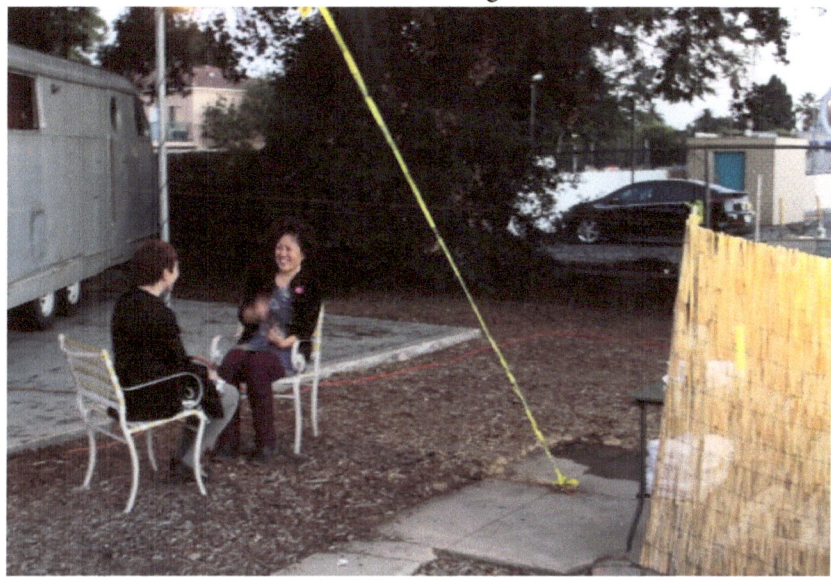

We had our sink under the tree for seven years. We hosted a series of artist projects, about 4 a year, and some of them were under the tree. There is one installation that is buried there, by artist, Barry Markowitz. When we had the Psychic Barber project, we had the hair-washing-station, and a place for the Psychic Readings. Above is a photo of one of the Psychic Readings.

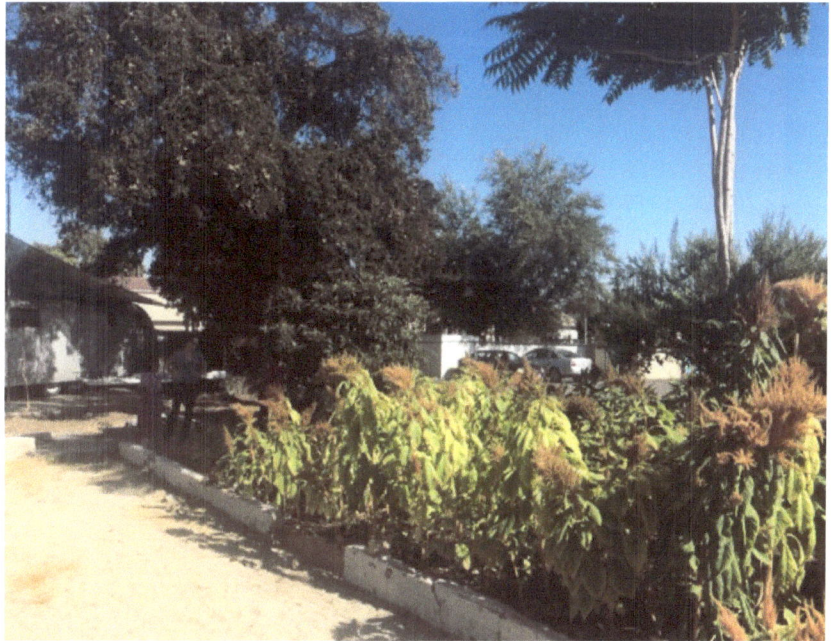

We also once grew a field of amaranth with the help of some farmers from Guatemala.

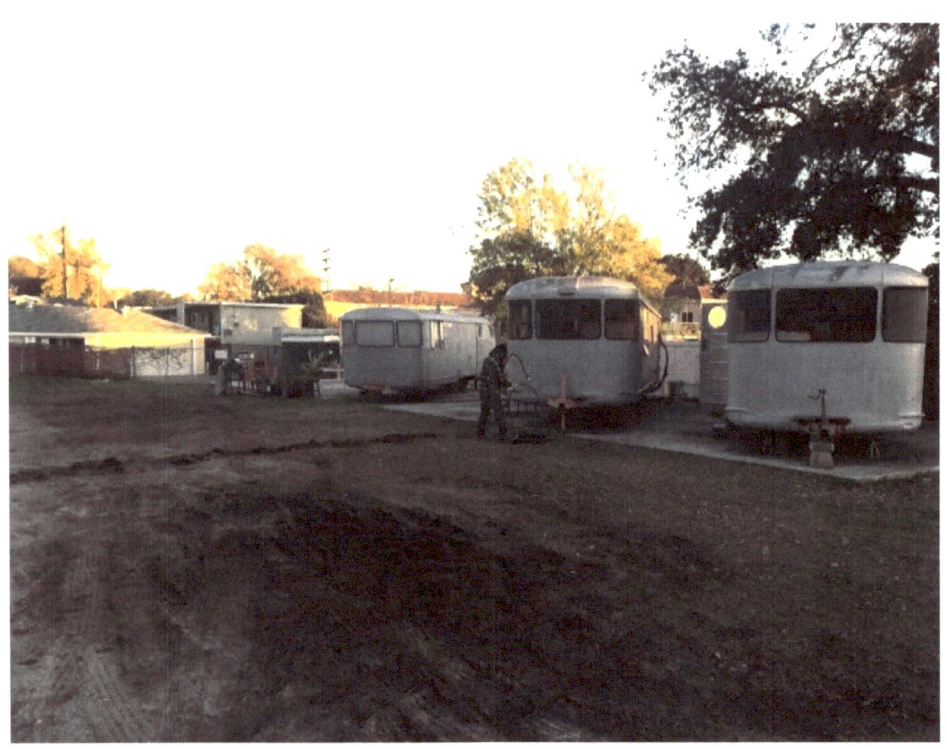

This is a photo of the trailers that were parked under the oak tree before our move to our new location. They are from Left to Right: 1949 Spartan Mansion, 1953 Spartan Imperial Mansion, 1949 Spartan Royal Mansion. We also have a mobile woodworking program that teaches tool use, design and fabrication to youth all over LA County. Our mobile classrooms were not parked under the tree since they went in and out every day, but they were in the vicinity.

Westminster Presbyterian Church

Painting is such a joy. One of the best ways to paint is with a group. I painted this while in a group of painters. I walked the whole church looking for an oak. This oak is at the side entrance. Imagine how many folks of Pasadena have walked under this oak on their way to prayer.

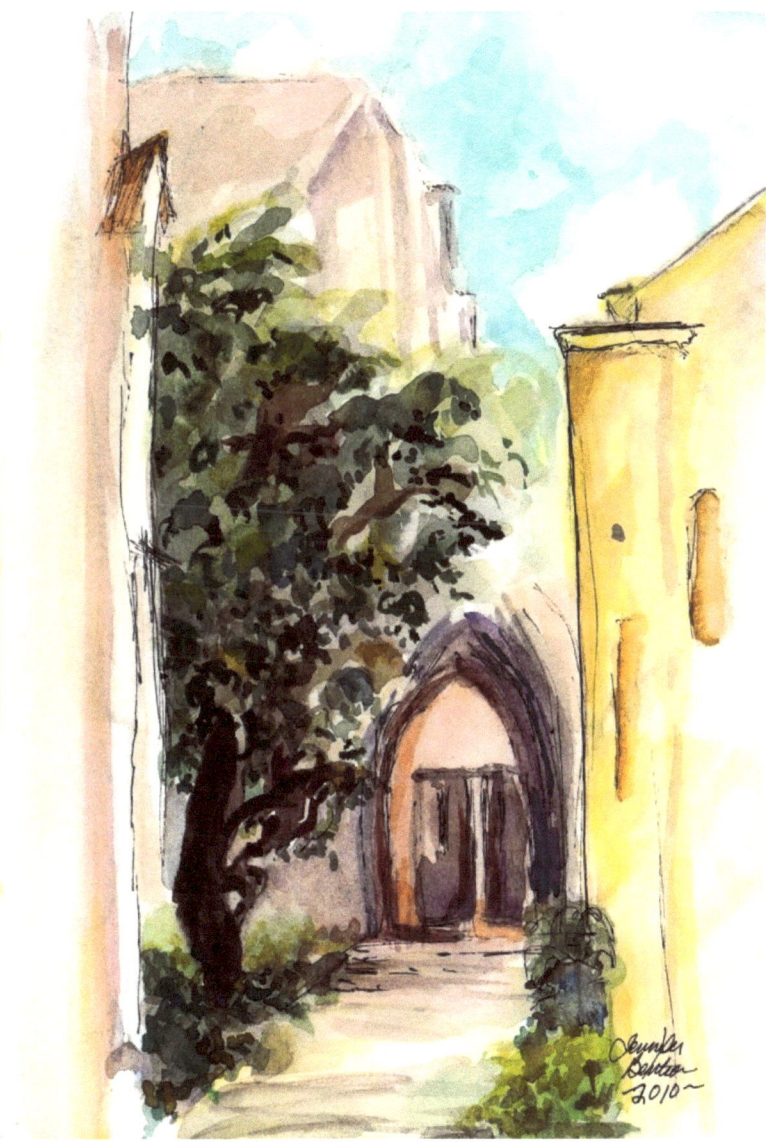

Open for Prayer, by Jennifer Bentson, 7" x 10", Watercolor

Painted on location

COUNCIL DISTRICT SIX

I have never visited the Pasadena Museum of History, yet I drive by it almost every day. It is located on the corner of Walnut and Orange Grove. I wanted to see if there were any books on the history of Pasadena that included oaks. The book store volunteer directed me to visit the reference library downstairs.

There I learned quite a lot from the staff about some historical oaks. Pasadena is so very rich with the fabric of history in its flora.

Adolphus Busch lived in Pasadena. He must have liked gardens because he started a garden at the bottom of the Arroyo. This was the first Busch Gardens. If you look at a map, there is a Busch Lane near the edge of the Arroyo.

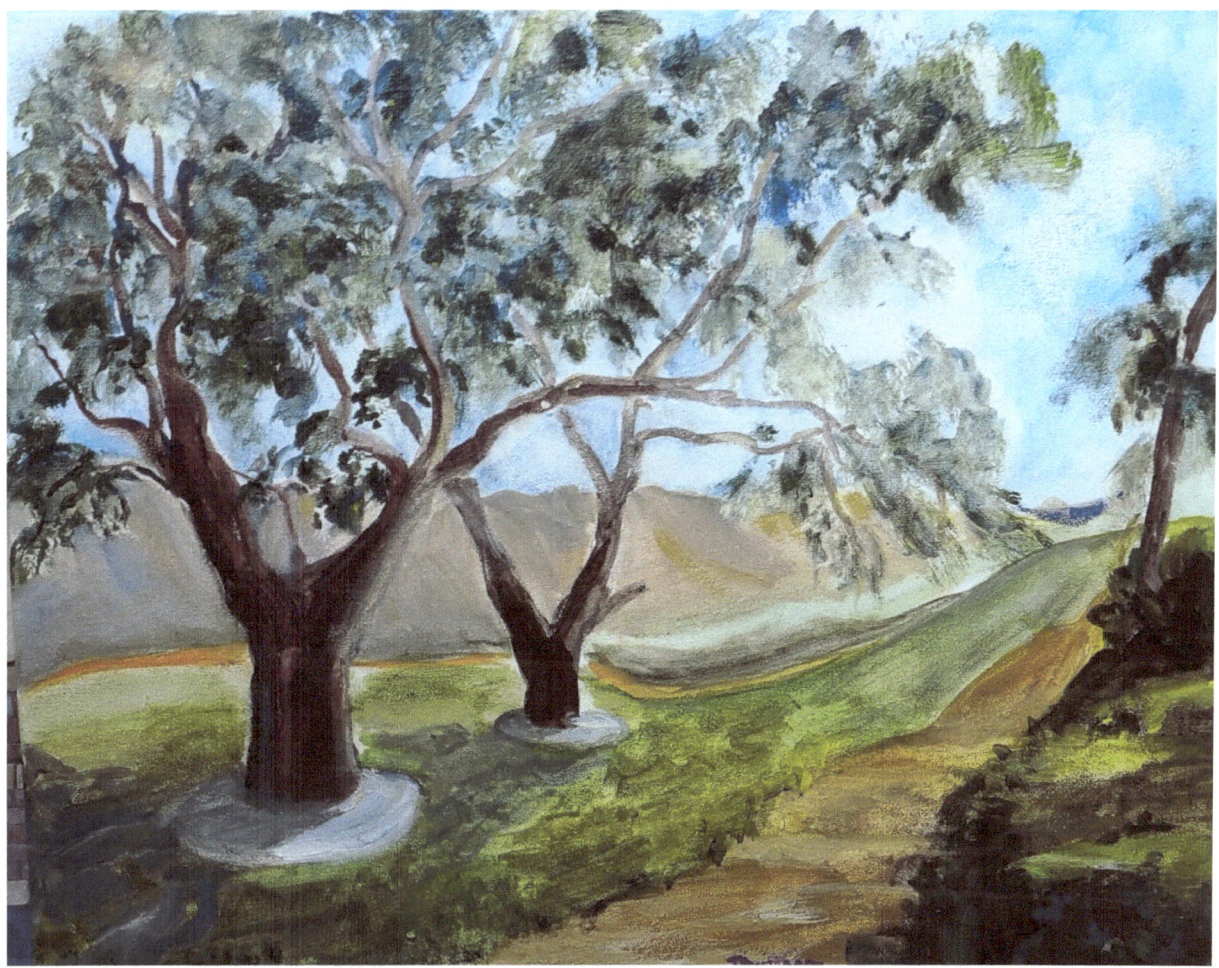

Busch Garden Oaks, by Jennifer Bentson, 16"x20", Oil

Painted in my studio

A Tale of Two Trees

By Kirk Myers

Pasadena has long been noted for its beautiful tree-lined streets, but the original landscape was a largely treeless plain, with a few native live oaks. The location of two of those trees determined the course of Orange Grove Avenue, when the land that later became West Pasadena was subdivided in early 1874.

Unlike the north-south direction of Fair Oaks Avenue, which then formed the eastern boundary of the settlement, Orange Grove Avenue inclined several degrees to the west. It was laid out to include two native live oak trees in the middle of the street, one at California and another one further south near State Street.

Both of the trees were often photographed, but the one at the intersection of Orange Grove and California seems to have achieved more recognition. On October 11, 1884 the Pasadena & Valley Union carried the following in the "Local News and Notes" section:

"Mr. E.F. Hurlbut has forwarded $5.00 to Thos. Nelmes, as his donation towards the rustic seat around the grand old Oak Tree on Orange Grove avenue. Mr. Nelmes informs us that he now has more than enough funds to erect this seat, which will be forty feet in circumstance (sic) and an attractive accommodation to travelers. …We presume this spot will someday be like unto the ancient forum at Rome, where the philosophers and orators of Pasadena may come to discuss the questions of the day."

In the book, Talking About Pasadena, early resident Benjamin McAdoo recalled how the tree was viewed by the community:

"In the middle of the street, California and Orange Grove, there was a large oak tree. It was right in the middle of the intersection. That oak tree was pampered and petted for years and years. They tried to keep it alive. It became very famous. It was written about and 'poemed' about all over the country, that oak tree that stood there."

The Pasadena Museum of History is located at the corner of Orange Grove Boulevard and Walnut Street (470 W. Walnut, Pasadena 91103); free parking in the Museum lot. The Research Library & Archives are open to the public free of charge Thursdays-Sundays from 1:00-4:00 pm. For additional information, please visit the Museum's website, www.pasadenahistory.org , or call 626-577-1660, ext. 10.

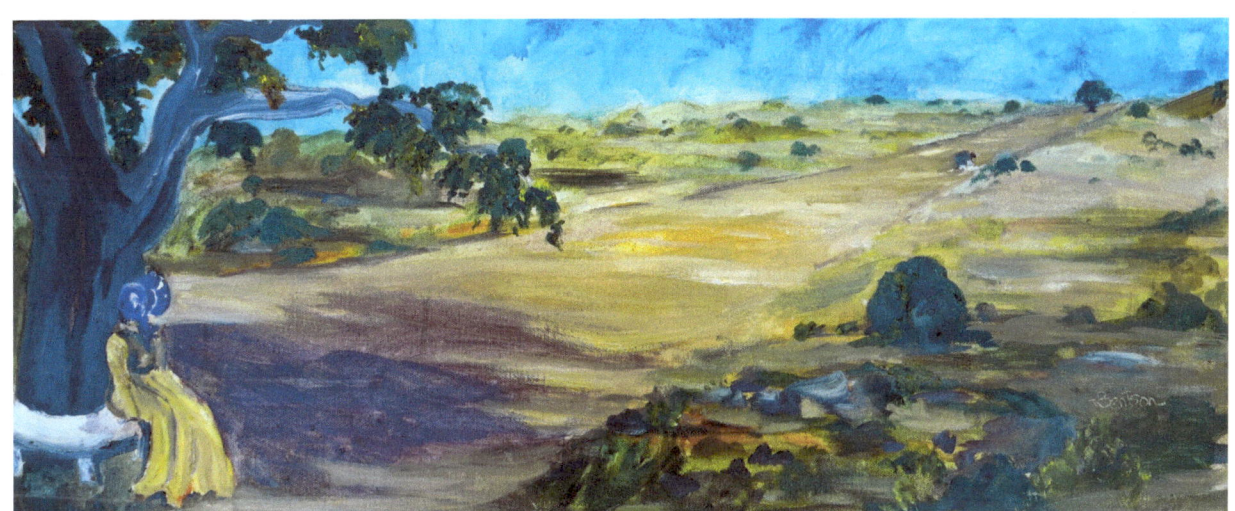

A Tale of Two Trees, by Jennifer Bentson, 12" x 30", Oil

Painted in studio.

La Loma Street Bridge Oak

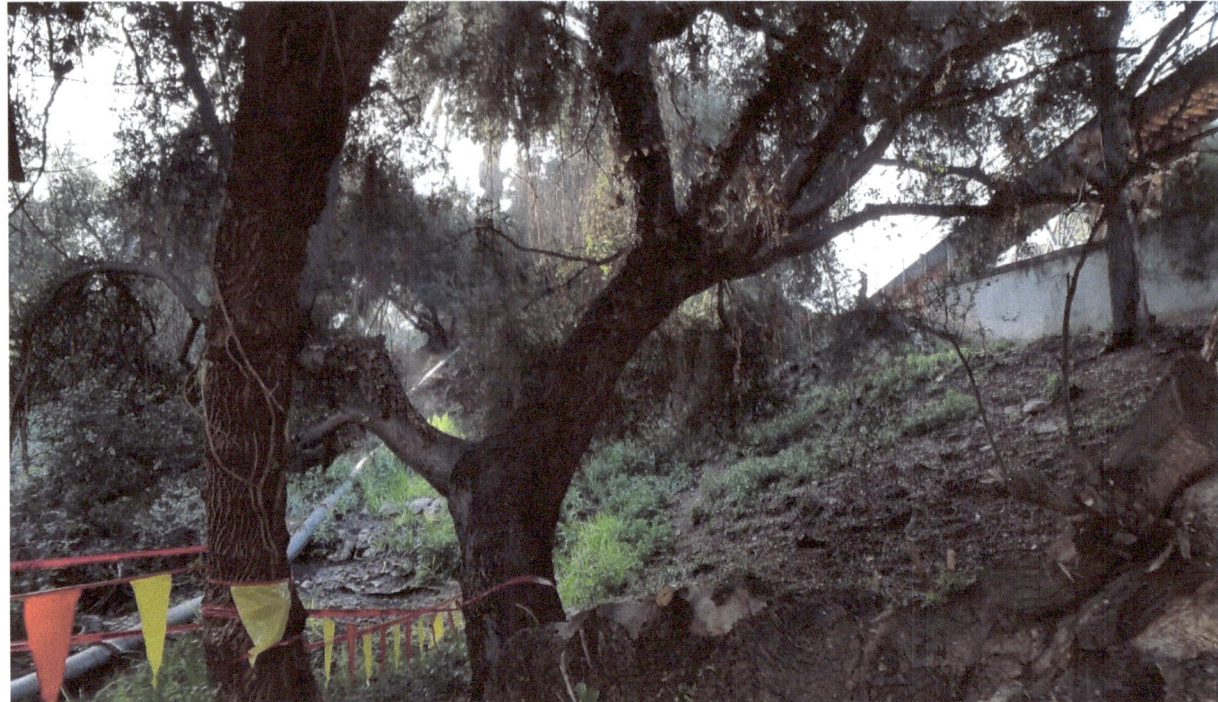

La Loma Street Bridge Oak, by Jennifer Bentson, Photograph

As we age, so do our bridges.

The La Loma Bridge is undergoing extensive reinforcement. I loved walking along the Arroyo to capture this oak tree. Darya Barar identified this tree as one of Pasadena's significant oaks. I think this picture shows the lengths that Pasadena goes to protect her oaks. The tree is cordoned off and construction "do not enter" tape was along the path. There was a huge crane parked just a few feet from this tree and you can see the bridge and La Loma Ave. in the upper right corner.

My father was a Structural Engineer. This means I grew up in a world that was mathematically correct and concrete, literally. Early in his career, my father, Raymond, assisted in the design of the Big Tujunga Bridge through LA County. He left the LA County employ and worked at Fluor Corporation for a while. Then I was born. He went back to LA County to pass out cigars. His friends suggested he file for a job in Plan Checking. He did and remained there for almost 30 years. As a very small child, I remember the cement trucks lining the Tujunga Canyon Road as we watched the pour of cement for his bridge. My father had a passion for concrete and there are many stories about that!

He passed away just a few months before this painting. I think his spirit wanted me to paint a bridge.

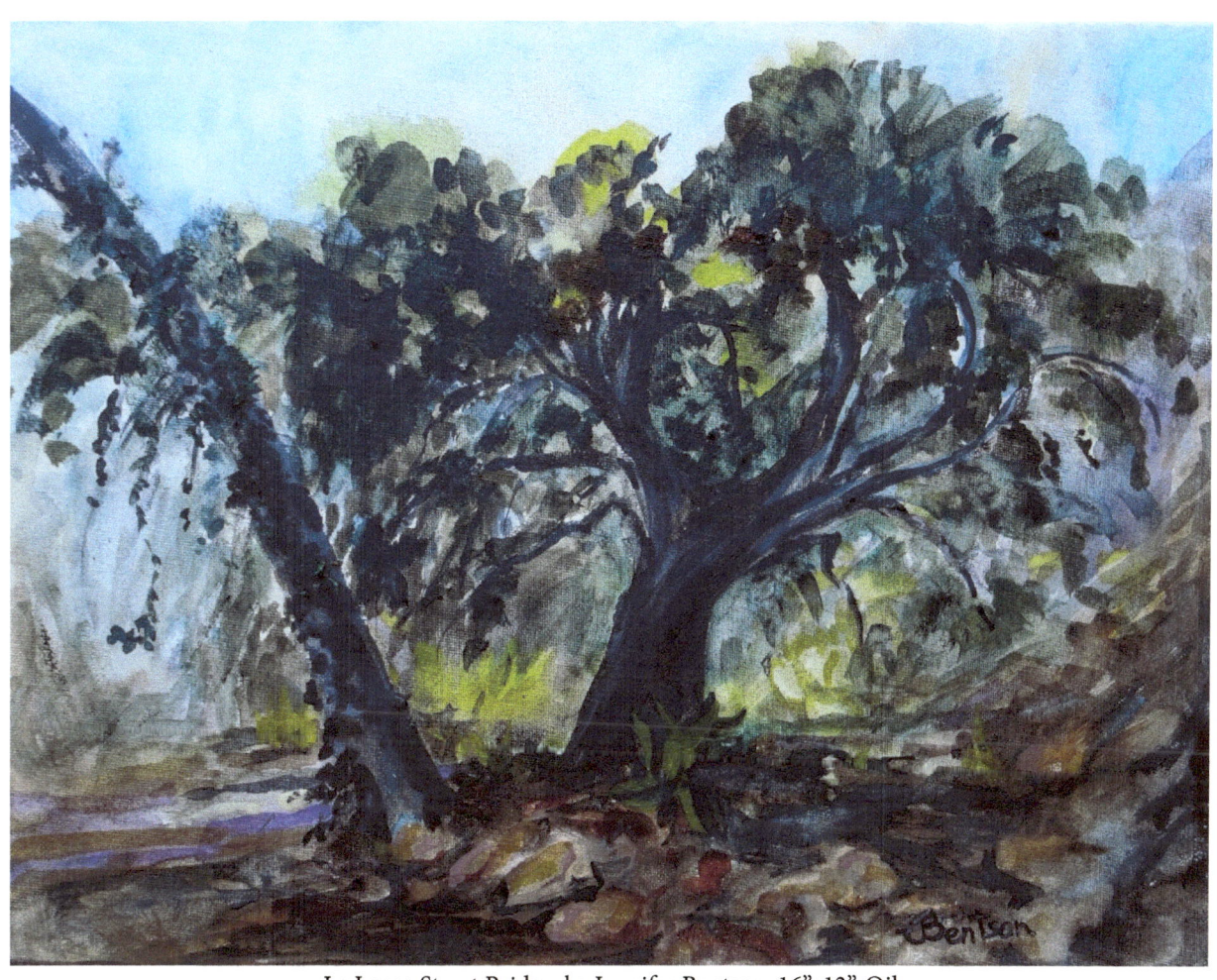

La Loma Street Bridge, by Jennifer Bentson, 16"x12", Oil

Painted on site

On the Edge of World Wide Church of God

I have two very close friends, Bin Hong from Malaysia and Paul Rieger from Russia. They are married. Paul Rieger worked at the Air Resources Board and was my husband's first boss. Bin Hong and Paul met at the World Wide Church of God when they were in college. Bin Hong had moved to Pasadena because of the World Wide Church of God and her devotion to the church. I cherish my friendship with this couple. Once we traveled to Hawaii together and while our husbands were busy together, Bin Hong and I decided to try a Mai Tai at every restaurant in Kona, Hawaii. Luckily at that time there were not too many restaurants. I think we made it to three restaurants. My favorite Mai Tai was from Bubba Gumps, it was blended and the bartender gave me the recipe. Bin Hong liked the one from Wind and Sea and told me that there is one in California in Dana Point. So now she goes there often.

This painting is of an oak on the edges of the World Wide Church of God property. I think it is an Engelmann. The World Wide Church of God sold off most of the huge campus in Pasadena. The new developer is constructing condos to sell. Since I have been painting this tree over the last year, I have witnessed the construction of the condos.

I drove by this in April 2016, and the tree has been pruned. I hope that it will survive the construction and the encroaching buildings. Oak trees have sensitive roots that grow near the surface of the ground. The oak tree will die if there is too much weight on the roots. The tree has a long arm that reaches towards Orange Grove. I think the tree wants a better view of the Rose Parade.

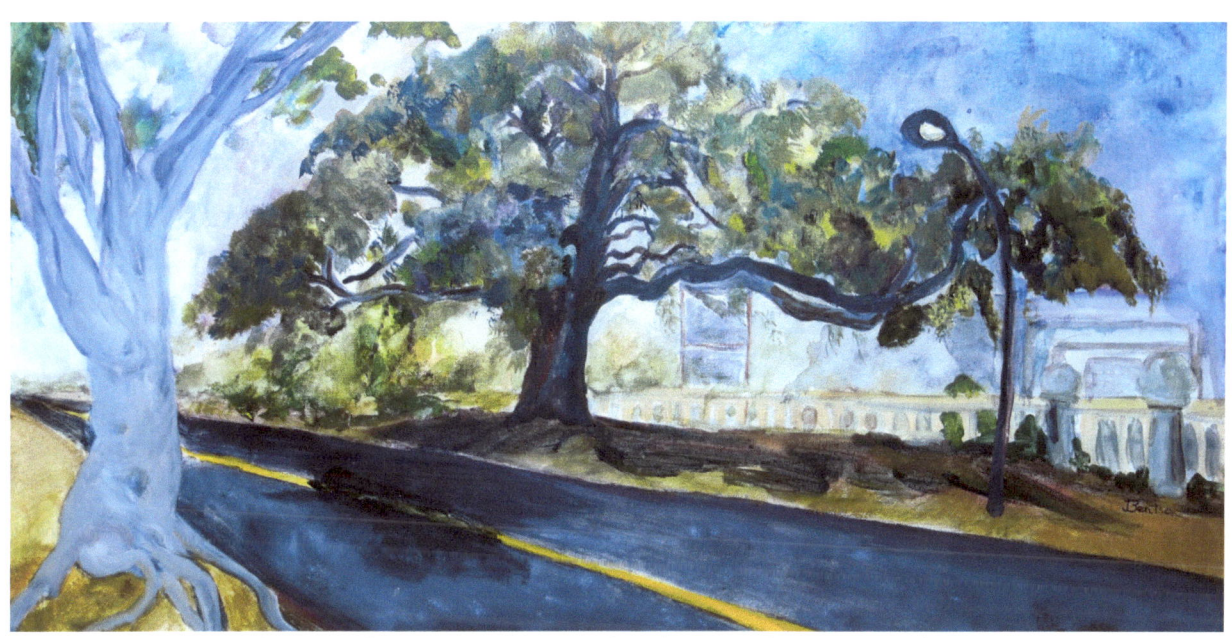

On The Edge of World Wide Church of God, by Jennifer Bentson, 36" x 18", Oil

Sketched on location and painted in the studio

Green Street Oak

My first love of painting was by necessity. I was in college at the University of Arizona and every weekend it seemed, I would go backpacking. Since I had to work to support my daily existence, I had no spare money for a camera. But I did have enough for a box of paints. I bought watercolors. They were the most portable of all the paints. I could carry the light paints in my backpack. It was a shame to go for miles and find that perfect vista without a camera. I would sit and paint the beauty of Arizona while resting from the exhausting hike.

I loved to climb the steep mountains above Tucson, once getting caught in a snow storm at the top of the arduous hike to Mt. Lemmon. I spent a very cold and wet night on the ground in my "tube tent" which was no protection from the rain which soaked my sleeping bag. In the morning, the only road to the mountain was closed. I hiked to the road and waited. Hitch-hiking back then was not so uncommon. Someone driving a VW bug picked me up after an hour or so. I had started to shiver. I don't remember ever being so cold. Sadly the VW had no heat. I arrived home about two hours later and promptly went into hot water. Did I go hiking after that, you bet!

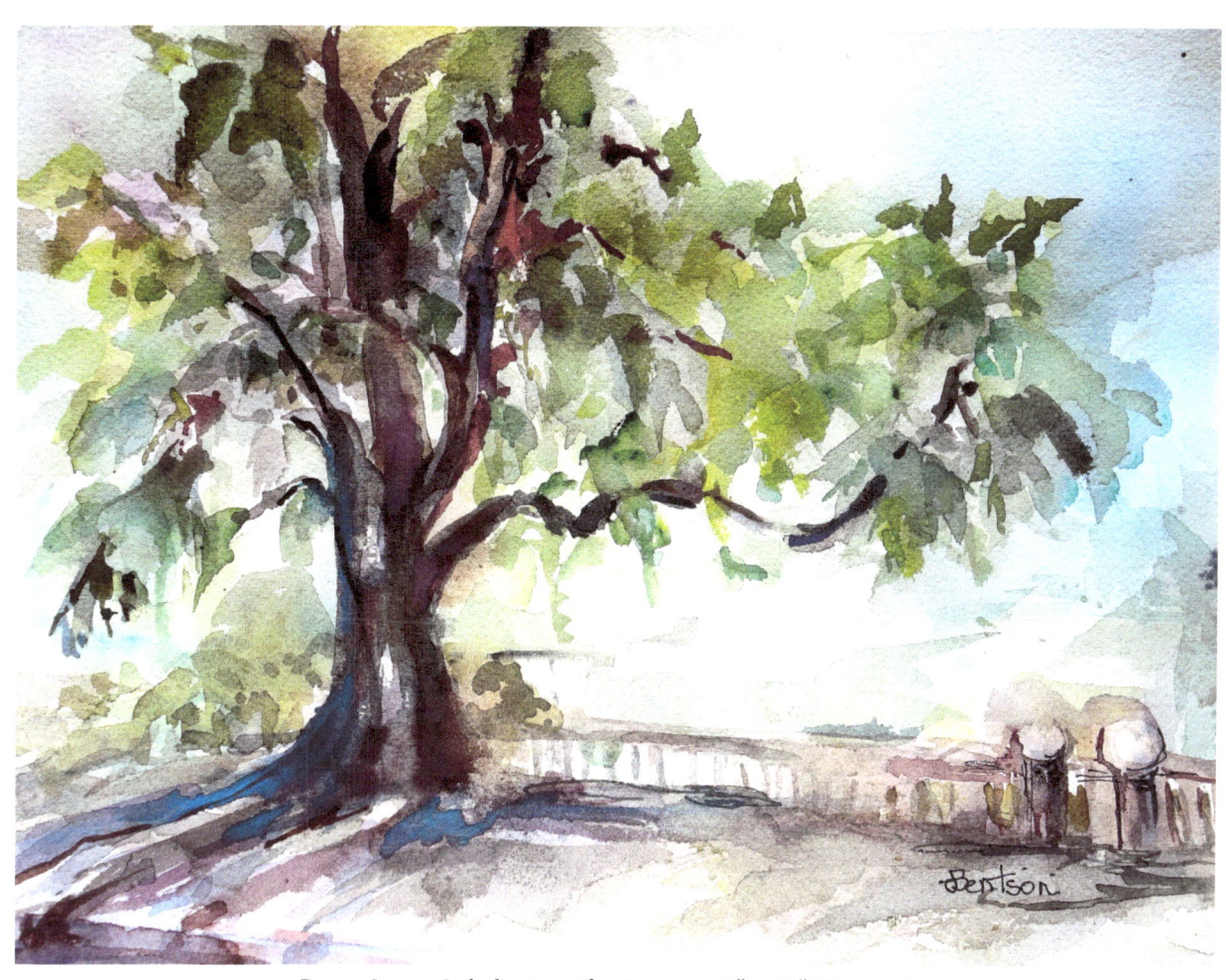

Green Street Oak, by Jennifer Bentson, 9" x 12", Watercolor

Painted on Location

COUNCIL DISTRICT SEVEN

My project, "California Oaks as Art," is my journey through painting and sketching the oaks of California which I consider as treasures. Oaks are one of the most common native trees in our state. As of 2004, the oak is the national tree of the USA For me the oak, particularly the California Live Oak, is a tree of beauty.

I began my project with research on the Big List of Trees for the US and California. The largest Engelmann Oak is right here in Pasadena on California Avenue.

CALTECH OAK

I Googled and found that there is a large Engelmann Oak at Caltech which is on California Avenue. This has to be it. I contacted Caltech and visited their oak. Sadly, this oak is reaching the end of its life. Caltech asked me to paint this oak tree as a vital memory. This launched my series of paintings, California Oaks as Art, and gave me the impetus to write a grant to the City of Pasadena.

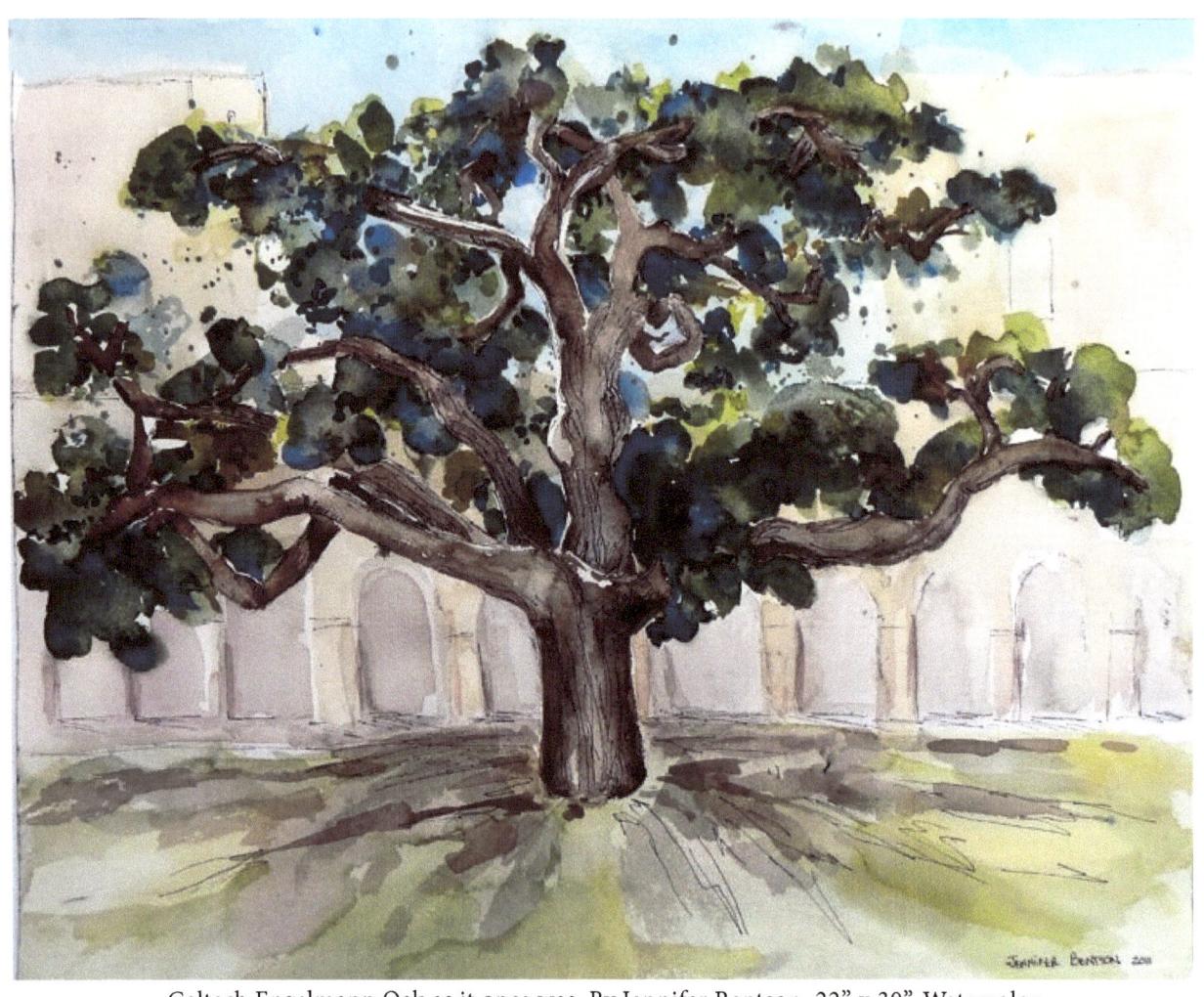
Caltech Engelmann Oak as it once was, By Jennifer Bentson, 22" x 30", Watercolor

Painted on location.

Preserving Caltech's *Engelmann* Oak Legacy

By Delmy Emerson and Charlotte (Shelley) Erwin of the Caltech Archives
With special acknowledgment to the Caltech Archives

The giant Engelmann Oak located on the Caltech campus along the arcade between Parsons-Gates and Dabney Hall sits almost directly in the center of the original 22-acre plot at the heart of the current campus. The original tract of land was gifted to Caltech, then Throop Polytechnic Institute by trustee, Arthur H. Fleming, in 1908. Shortly thereafter, the first building was constructed on ground just to the east of the majestic old oak. This was Throop Hall, then known as Pasadena Hall. The graded lawn in front of Throop was bounded by retaining walls topped with a balustrade and broken by double stairs going down to the lower ground. On the north side, this retaining wall wrapped around the old Engelmann Oak, linking it to the central building site.

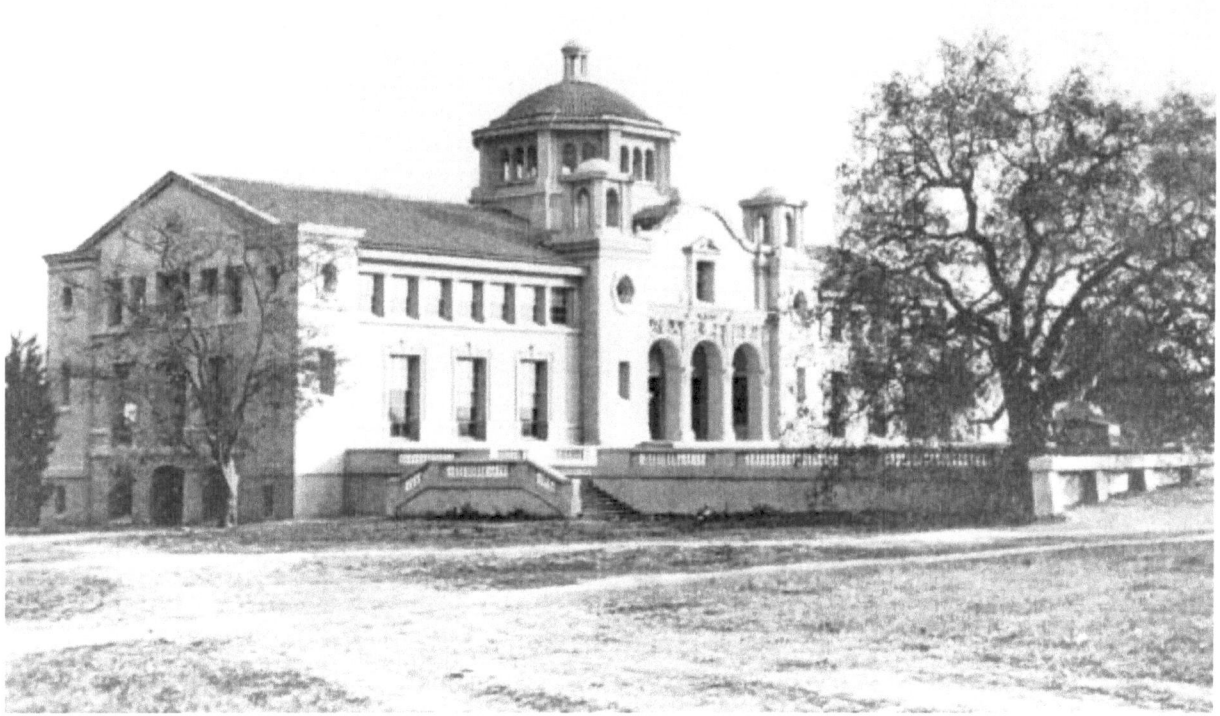

Throop Hall ca. 1910. Photo Courtesy of the Caltech Archives

The Engelmann Oak has survived Throop Hall, which was demolished following the 1971 San Fernando earthquake.

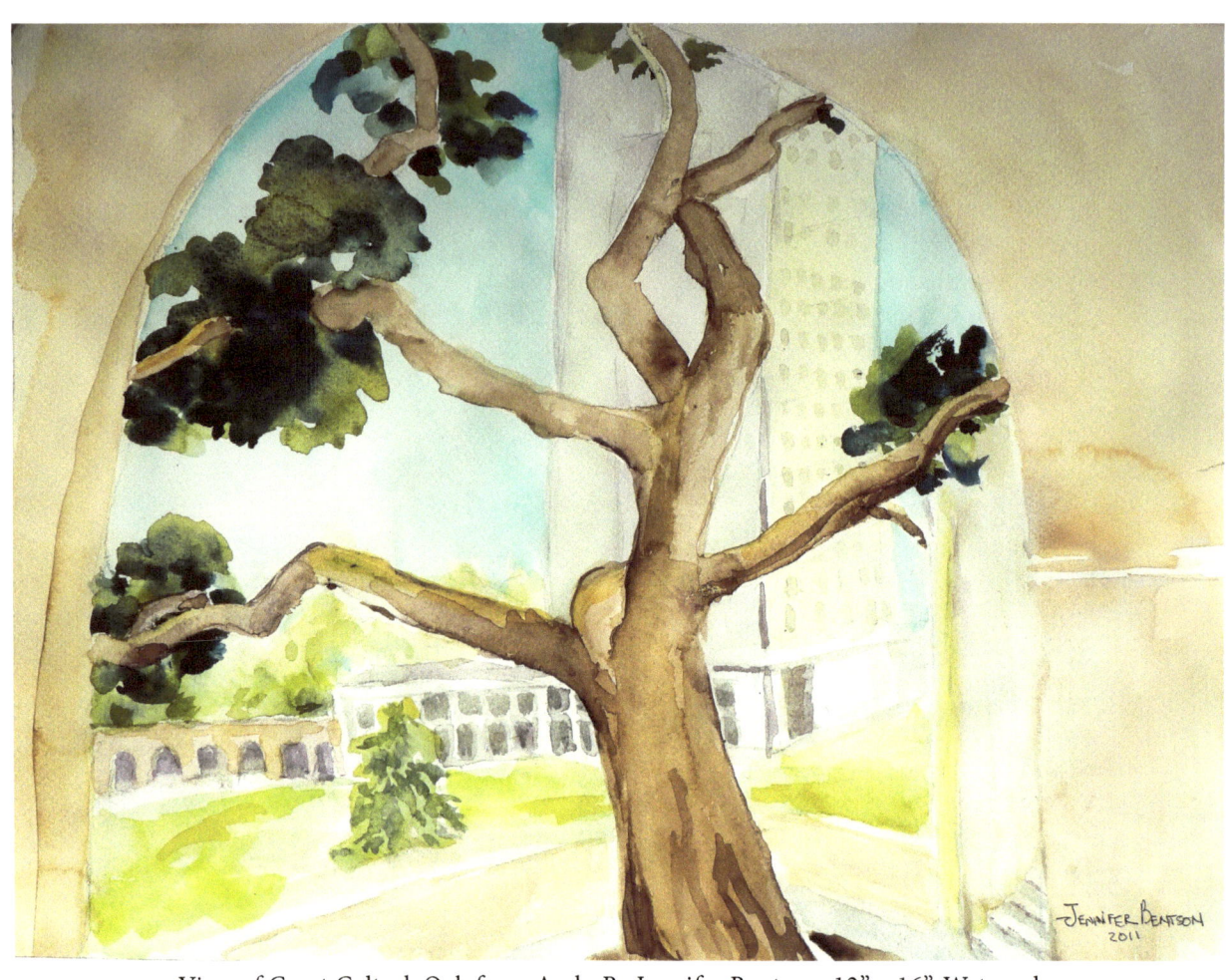

View of Great Caltech Oak from Arch, By Jennifer Bentson, 12" x 16", Watercolor

Painted on Location

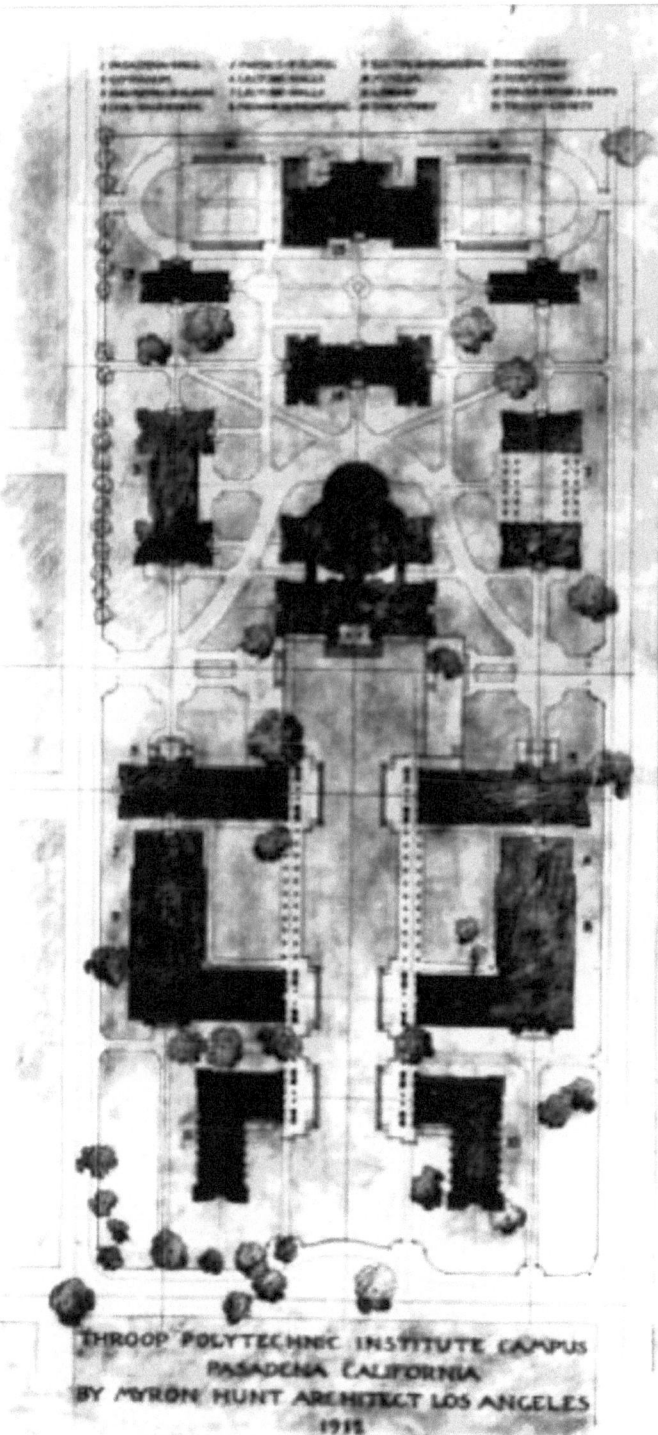

Hunt plot plan, 1912. Photo Caltech Archives

Beginning with Arthur Fleming, the early campus leaders were deeply conscious of the importance of maintaining the native flora of the site. Fleming, who held the position of chairman of the board of trustees from 1917 to 1933, was himself a lumberman and tree expert. By his own account there were forty California oaks of varying species on the plot in 1910. Later some of these would be removed to make room for buildings. The earliest plot plan, drawn up in 1912 by Myron Hunt, the architect who designed Throop Hall. It included a number of trees we would still recognize today, including the large Engelmann oak near the center.

Hunt did not complete his building program, but his plot plan was passed on to his successor, New York architect Bertram Goodhue. In a letter to Goodhue of October 1915, Throop's president, James A. B. Scherer, called particular attention to the campus oaks: "They are live oaks, and in this semi-tropical country each live oak is regarded as an invaluable asset on a given piece of property. ... In other words, these trees should virtually govern the lay-out of the buildings."

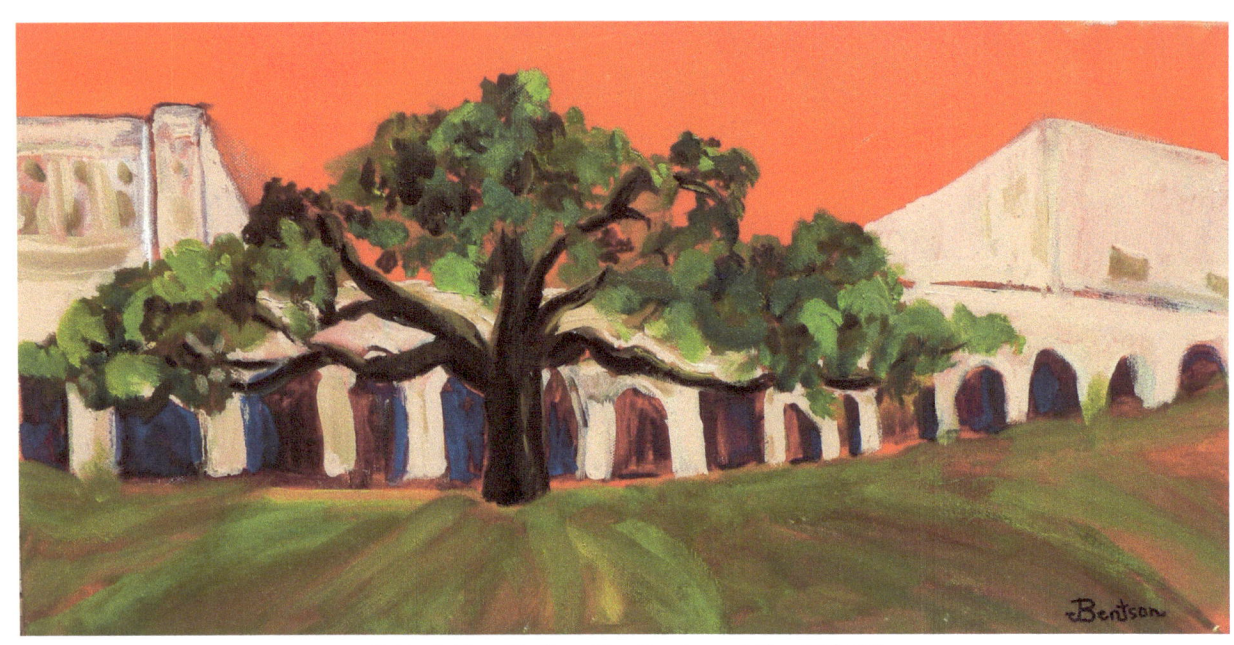

Caltech Hot, By Jennifer Bentson, 24" x 12", Oil

Painted in Studio

It was not until 1928 and the building of Dabney Hall, the fifth building on campus (after Gates, Bridge and Sloan laboratories), that thought was given to obtaining the services of a landscape designer for the creation of Dabney Garden. This was Beatrix Farrand, the wife of Max Farrand, then the director of the Huntington Library. After the completion of Dabney, the arcade or "portales" linking Gates and Dabney was created, creating the present-day backdrop to the old Engelmann Oak.

In the spirit of President Scherer, Mrs. Farrand argued for a unified landscape plan guided by the existing trees. She wrote in March 1928 to Arthur Fleming: "The whole campus should be so obviously a unit, with its oaks and carefully chosen groups that the treatment should be carefully thought out and planned for density and mass effect, and the various courts should be worked out as parts of the design." Dabney Garden, the first "court," was planted with olive trees, as was the later Olive Walk, designed by another landscape architect, Florence Yoch, in the early 1930s. Farrand continued to work on landscaping until 1938 and oversaw the planting of several oaks in the neighborhood of Arms and Robinson laboratories. In 1939, a California native plant garden was established with the help of Theodore Payne. That garden stood until the building of Church Laboratory in 1955. A campus scene from 1935 shows Throop Hall's west façade and Gates Laboratory to the left, with the huge old Engelmann Oak still anchoring the center of campus. Campus view from the top of Robinson, 1935.

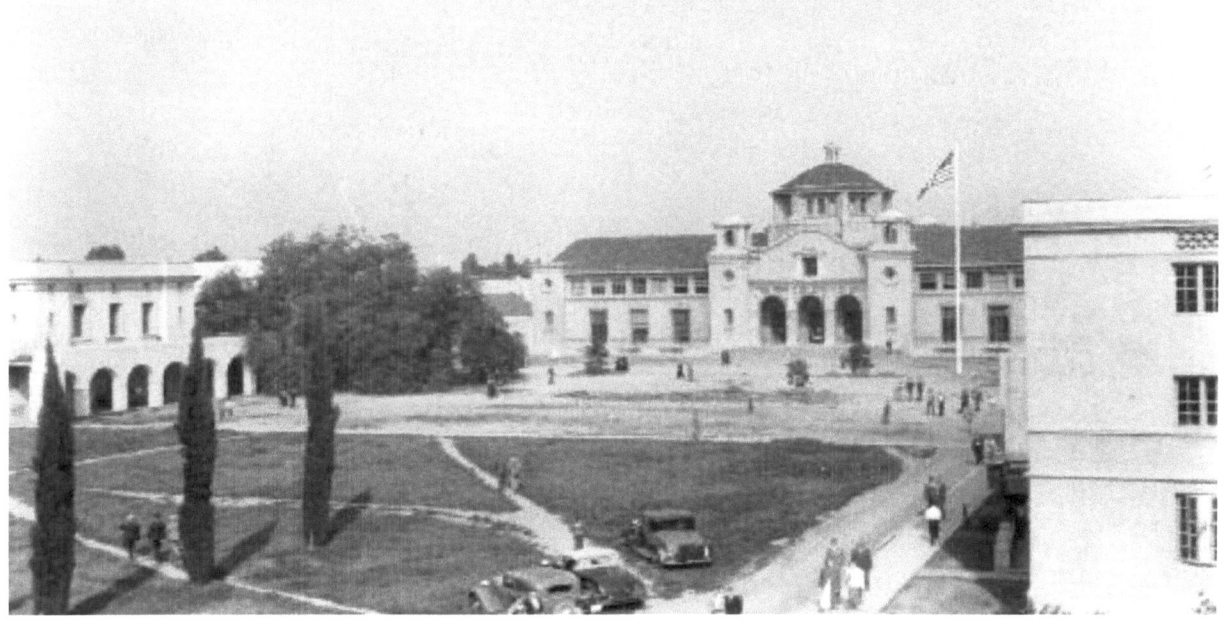

Photo Caltech Archives

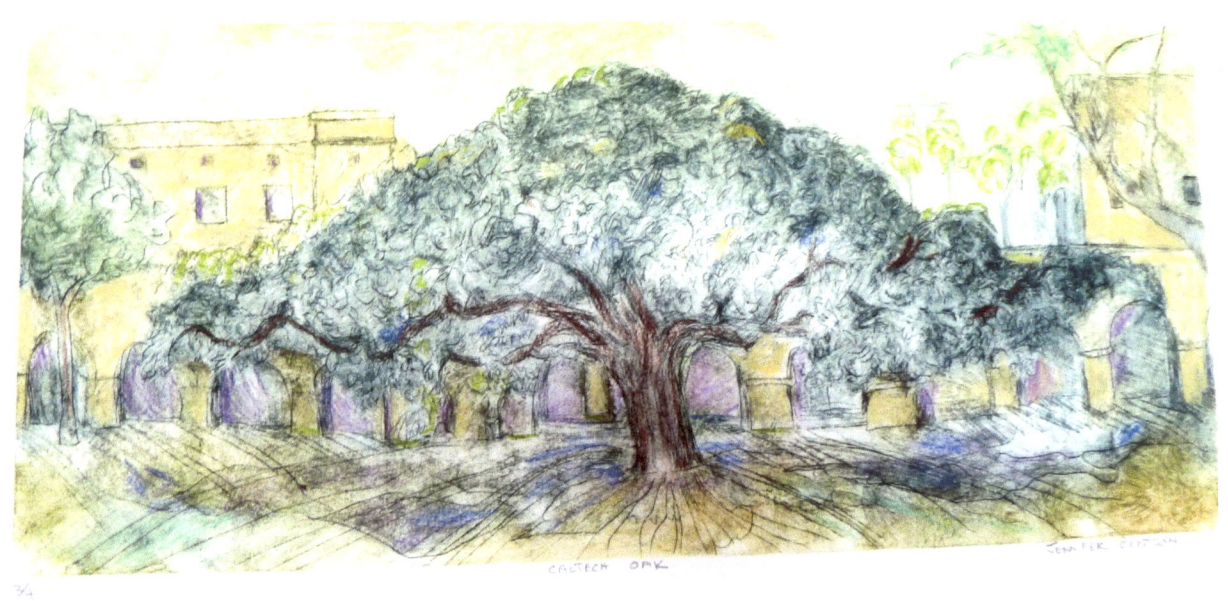

Caltech Engelmann Oak in Full Canopy, By Jennifer Bentson, 17.5" x 5.5" Dry Point Print

Printed in the Wong Shue Print Studio

Fast forward to 1979. A campus planning report presented a table of "Campus Plant Material," listing three species of *quercus* (oak), all noted to be in "moderate" use. Ten years later, Caltech's [first?] master plan included a tree inventory listing 54 species of valuable specimen trees, of which six were California oaks. Thus three additional species were added in the intervening years. In order to preserve the Engelmann Oak collection on campus, in 2013 seed propagation was used to establish a tree sapling to help conserve the diminishing Engelmann Oak habitat throughout the Southern California area.

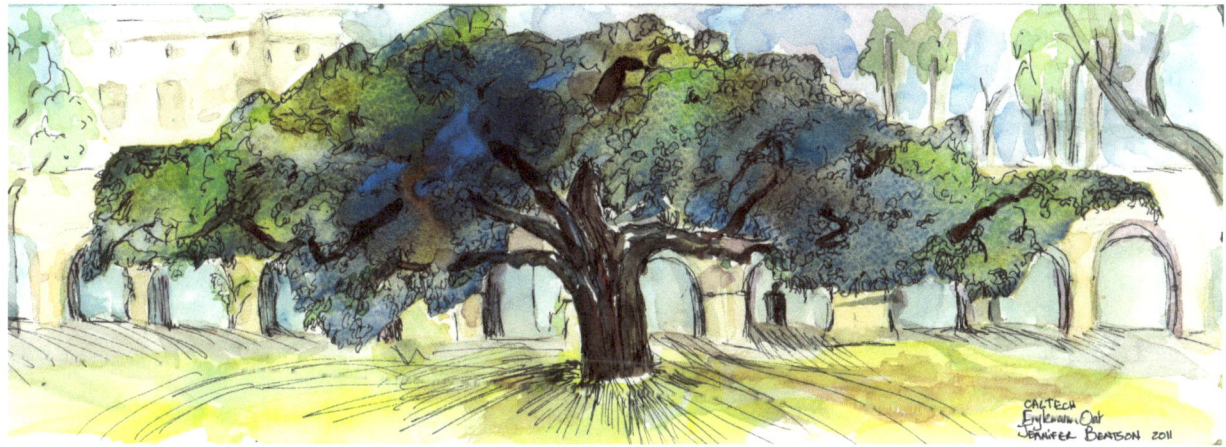

Caltech, Engelmann Oak By Jennifer Bentson, 17.5" x 6", Watercolor and Pen

Painted in Studio

"Meditation on a Garden"
By Jennifer Bentson

Paisley rays of sun coat my purpled life.
I turn with one simple movement
Silent, falling, reaching ecstatic planes, which contain…
Morose fields swamped with mud.
Cover me.

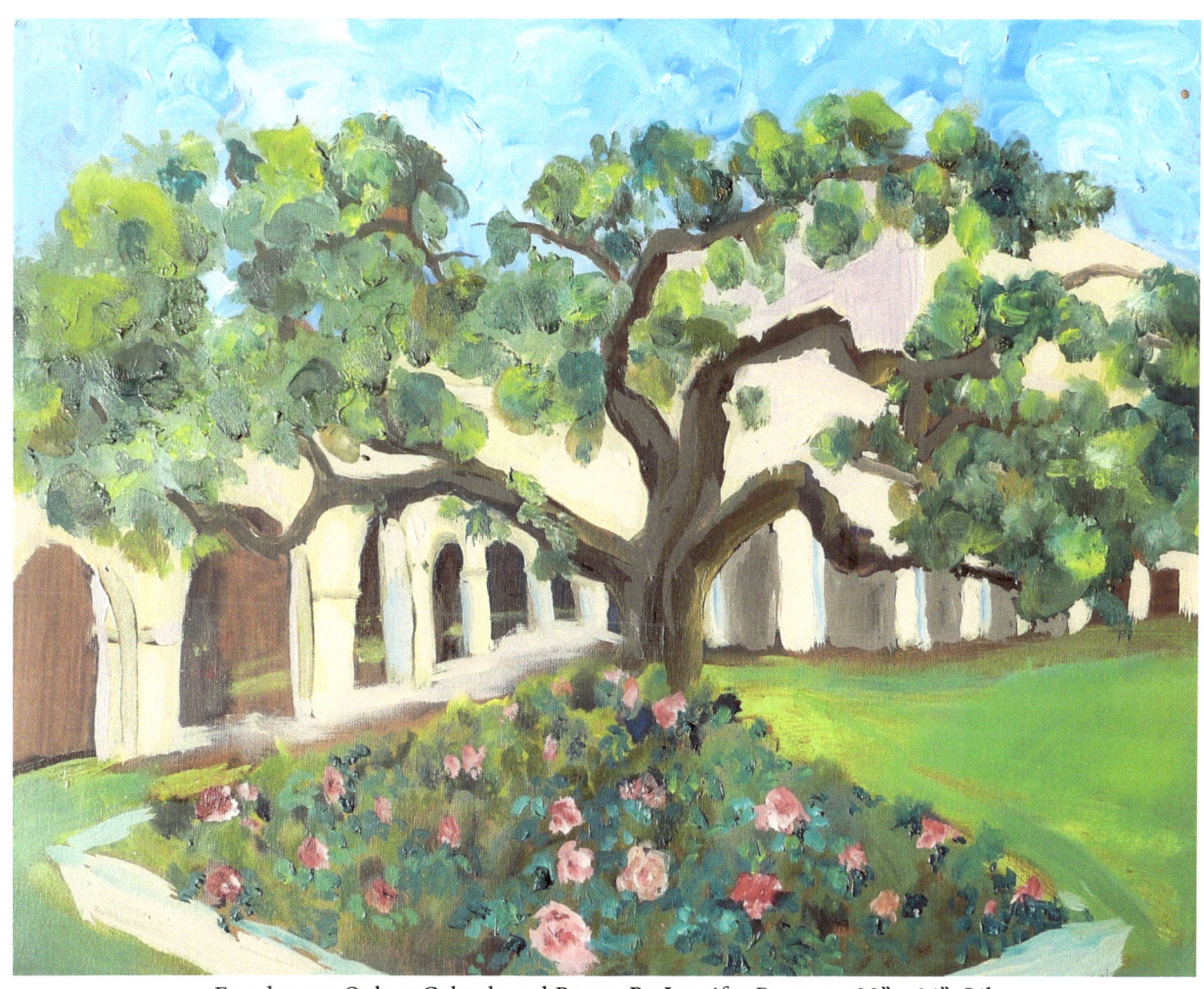
Engelmann Oak at Caltech and Roses, By Jennifer Bentson, 20" x 24", Oil

Painted in Studio

"History"
By Jennifer Bentson (1967)

The grains of time have washed away the feelings of the dawn.
The gentle touch of life exists though mists must be dawn.
And I, a meager whim crash violently to shore.
Where grains of time receive the now
With grains of time before.

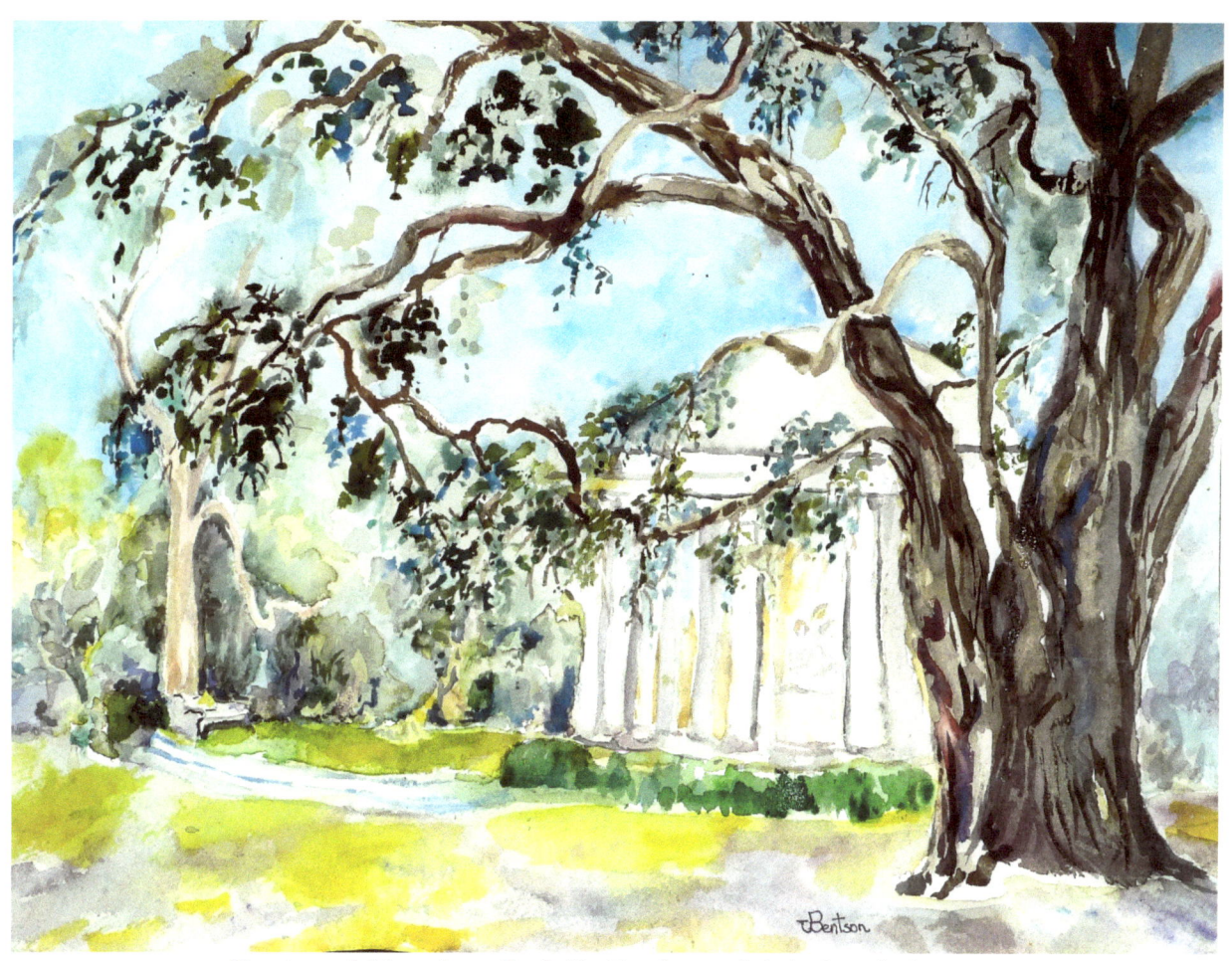

Huntington's Mausoleum Shaded by Engelmann Oak, by Jennifer Bentson,

Painted on Location at Huntington Gardens

Huntington Library, Art Collections, and Botanical Gardens

The Garden Curator told me about the oaks at Huntington Library, Art Collections, and Botanical Gardens. I joined the gardens as a member and learned about the special group of artists allowed to paint there. I went through the interview process, signed an agreement and was given a pass to paint in the gardens on the day it is closed. This offered such a wonderful opportunity to wander through the gardens, drinking up all the vistas by myself. There is something soulful about the luxury of seeing nature without the clamor of the everyday activities of the gardens.

My first stop was the Canary Island Bed in the Succulent Garden. Honestly, I think I could live in a place that looked like this garden. The sculptural shapes of the succulents tickle an unseen part of me. It was Spring and the cacti were blooming. So I was able to sit and paint this oak tree quietly and in communion with the garden.

As an outdoor painter, the air, light and smell all go into my painting. It is why I prefer to be on location to paint. I prefer to use watercolors when I am on location. They are less invasive if the water should splash or spill. The pigments are minerals anyway, so they really are more environmentally safe than oils.

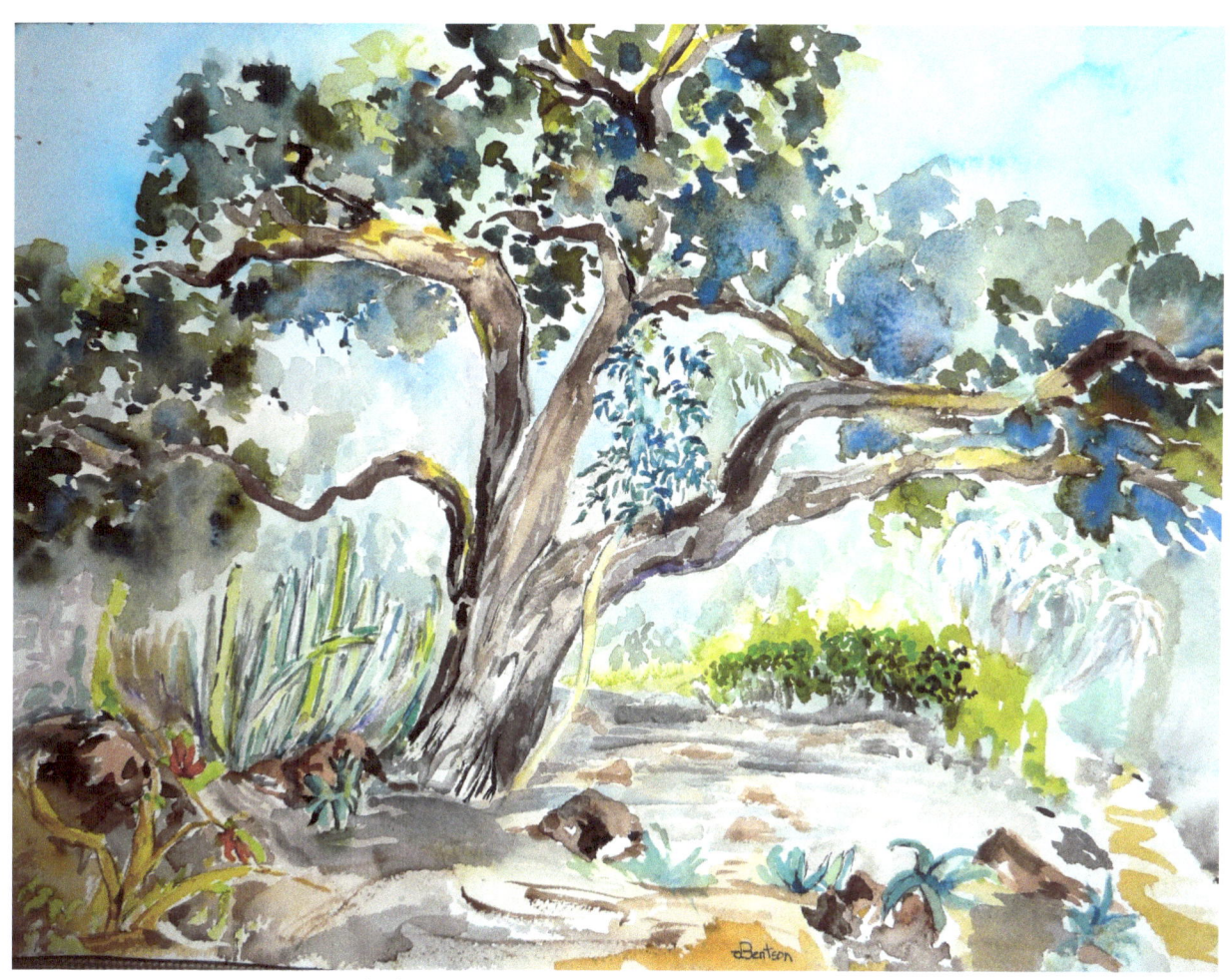
Huntington Garden's Canary Isle Oak, By Jennifer Bentson, 16"x12", Watercolor

Painted on Location

Lombardy Street Oak

Darya Barar of the City of Pasadena suggested I paint this oak as Pasadena built the street around the oak.

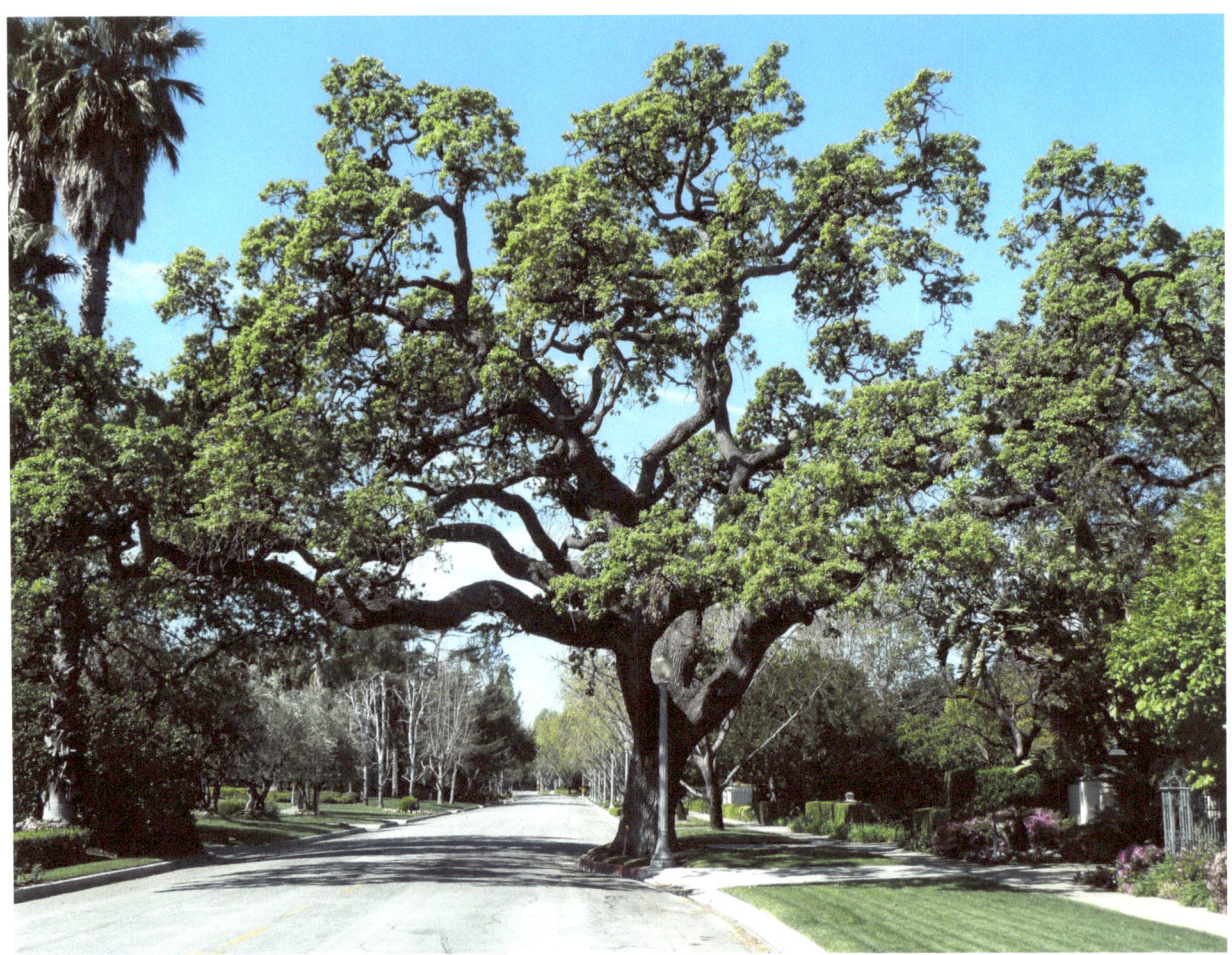

Lombardy Oak, By Jennifer Bentson, Photograph

I like the street light and the oak in conjunction. The City of Pasadena has made many efforts to preserve their oak heritage.

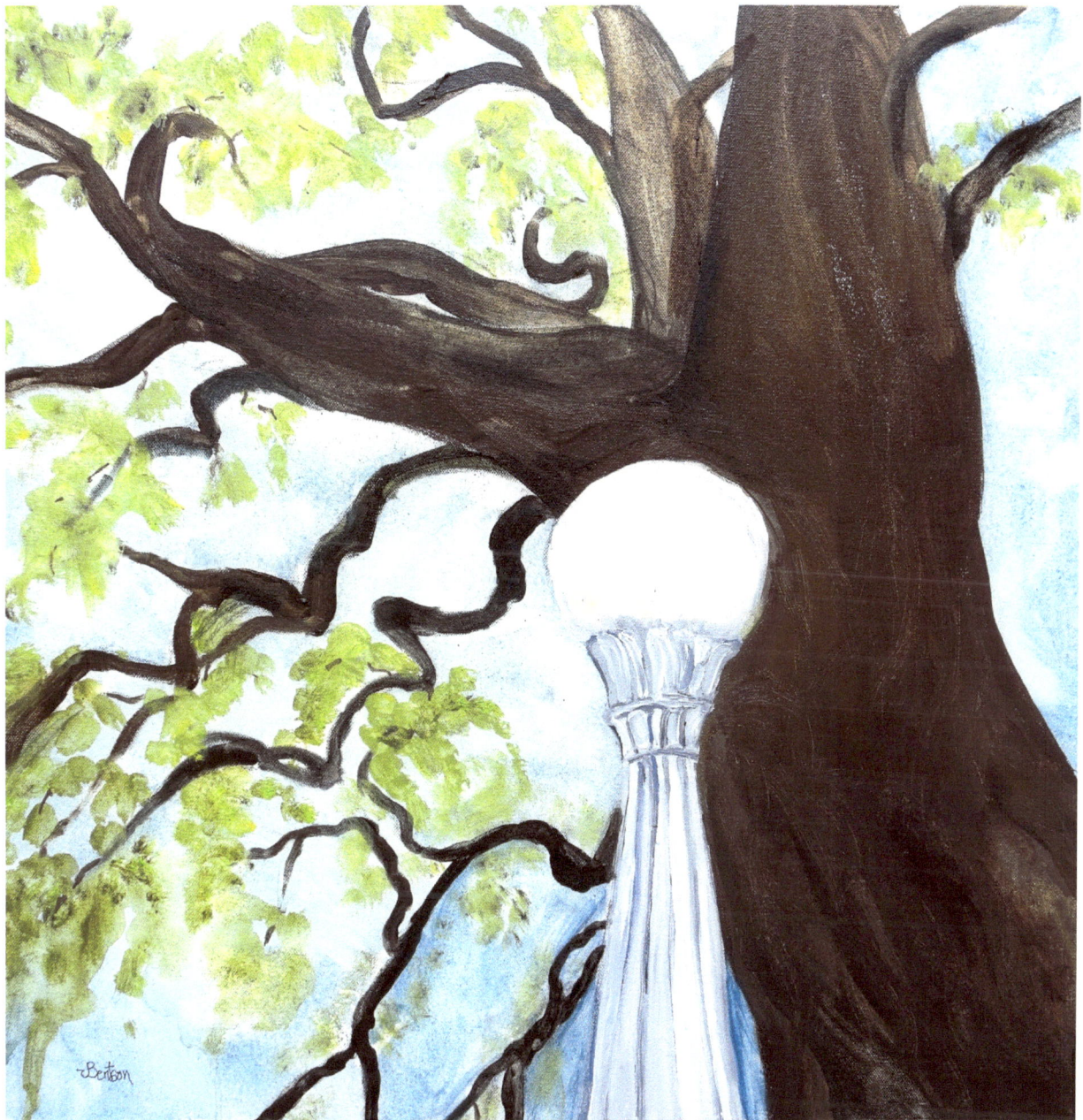

Lombardy Street Oak, by Jennifer Bentson, 24" x 24", Oil

This was sketched on location and painted in my studio.

Largest Englemann Oak in USA

The Big Tree List of California and the Big Tree List of the USA have the largest Engelmann Oak as in Pasadena, California. Originally, I thought the oak was the one at Caltech. I was surprised to learn that the largest Engelmann Oak recorded is at a private residence (not Caltech) on California Avenue. I contacted the owner who had the house up for sale. He granted me permission to paint this tree. This tree is in a hedge. Engelmann Oaks are not reproducing as well as the Coastal Oaks and are facing endangerment. The Arroyo Foundation, Pasadena Beautiful and local garden clubs are collecting acorns to foster more Engelmann Oak Trees.

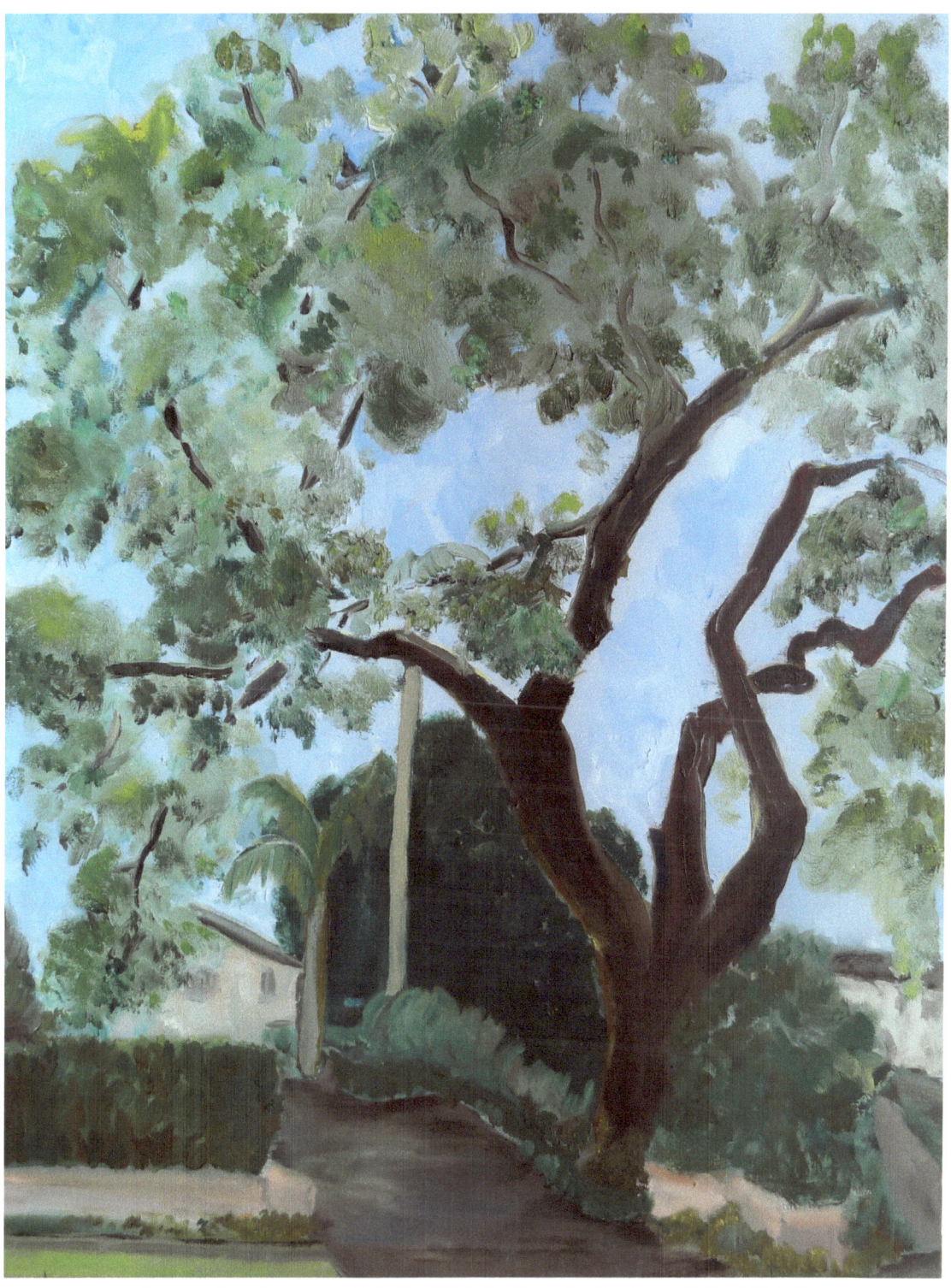

Largest Engelmann Oak in the USA, by Jennifer Bentson, 20" x 24", Oil

Painted on location

OAKS OUTSIDE OF PASADENA

ZORTHIAN RANCH

www.zorthianranch.com

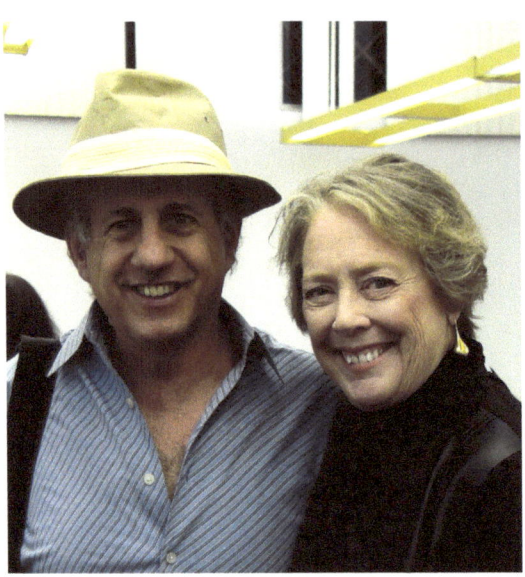

Alan Zorthian and Jennifer Bentson

This ranch is closely linked to Pasadena and the Art Community. Alan Zorthian is the son of Jirayr Zorthian, an artist, who emigrated to the U.S. after experiencing the Armenian Genocide. Jirayr Zorthian purchased the 48 acres of land adjacent to Pasadena. The Zorthian Ranch, as it is known today, is a creative center for the arts and local artists.

Alan Zorthian manages the ranch, which is often used for filming and is on the Air BnB list.

Alan remembers the times his father would entertain scientists from Caltech as well as musicians and artists. I learned that Charlie Parker once played at the ranch and slept in the building in my painting. Other famous personages visited the ranch as it was and is a hub for the creative spirit that flies over Pasadena.

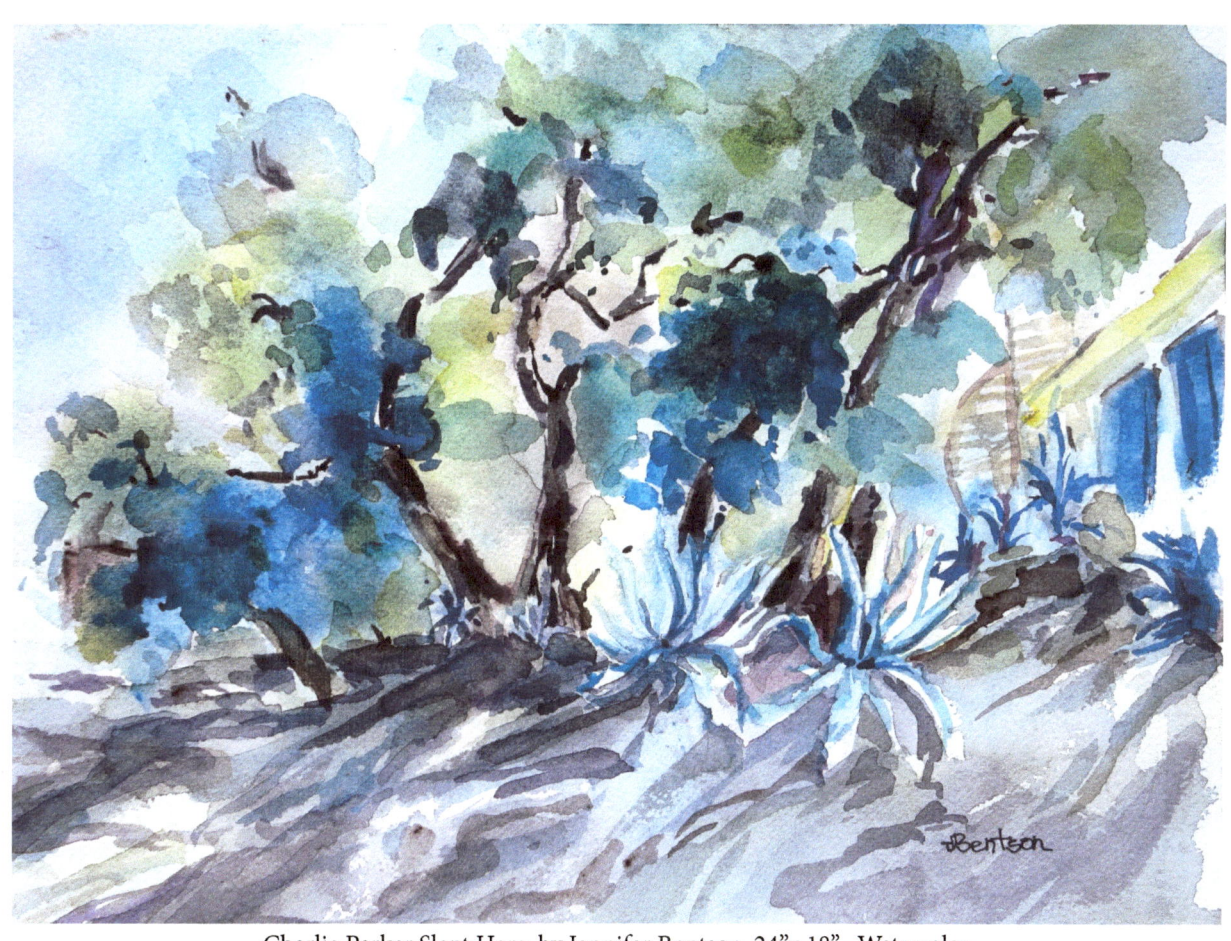

Charlie Parker Slept Here, by Jennifer Bentson, 24"x 18" , Watercolor

Painted on location with conversation from a 6 year old.

NUNCIO'S NURSERY

Grandfather Guilio Nuncio and Uncle Joe Nuncio started Nuncio's Nursery growing camellias and then added azaleas in their backyard in Alhambra. The business grew beyond the confines of the backyard. At the end of World War II in 1946, Grandfather Guilio bought a large parcel of land on Chaney Trail in Altadena where Tom, Jim, Julius and Julius have tended and cultivated the camellias and azaleas.

When Grandfather first moved to the Chaney Trail location he had land but there was no water supply for the thirsty plants. The Nuncios contacted the local water company and learned that there was lots of water, but no pipe. Due to the war, metal and metal pipe was not to be found for purchase anywhere. Using the help of local characters who operated off the grid, so to speak, metal pipe was delivered to the nursery in a matter of days for the cost of a case of whiskey. No questions asked.

Now Nuncio's has developed hundreds of varieties of camellias and azaleas. There is estimated to be about 300,000 plants at the nursery. Many of the plants are under the oak trees. Interestingly, there are not too many plants that will thrive under an oak tree. Camellias and azaleas are two that grow fearlessly.

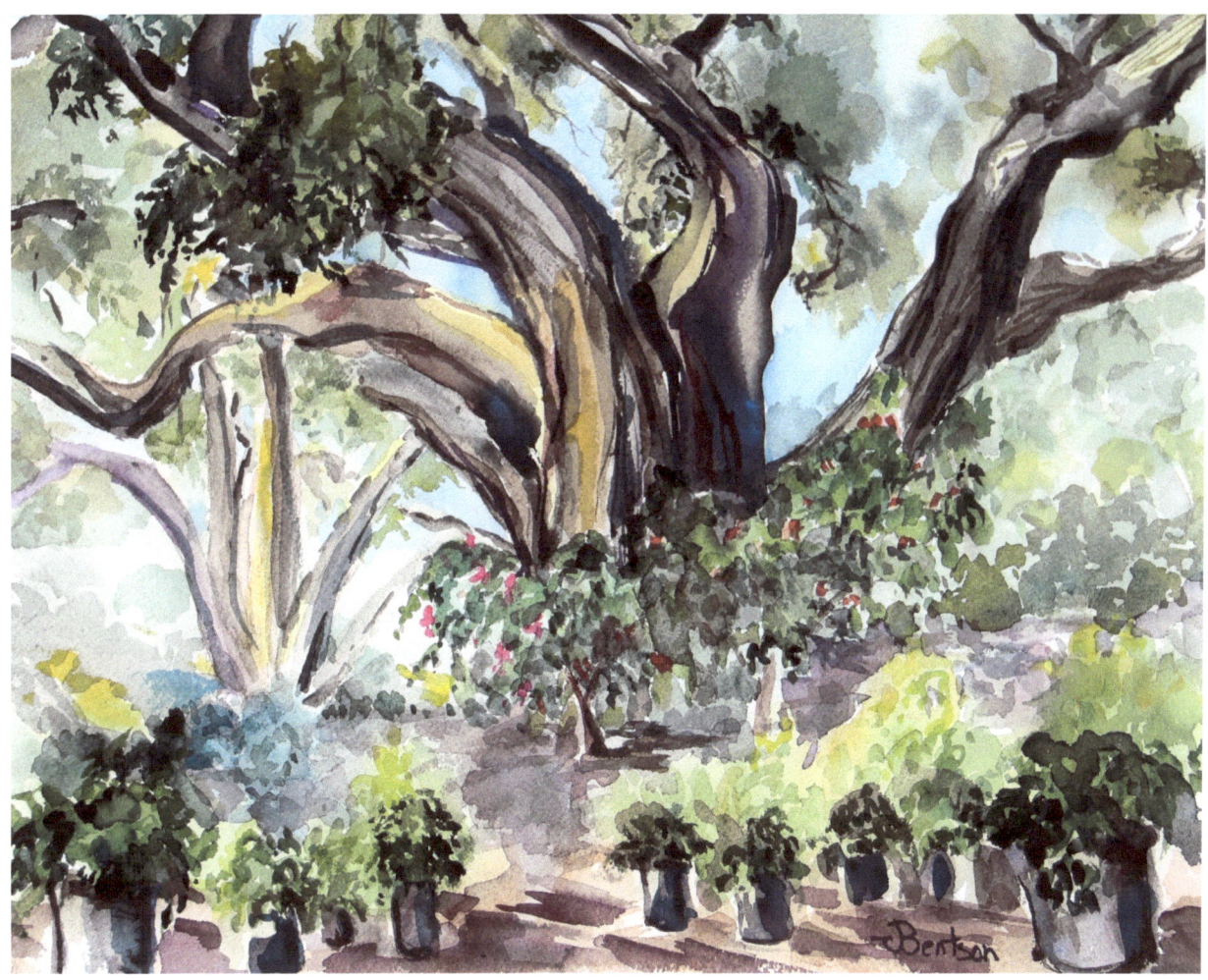

Under the Oaks at Nuncio's Nursery, by Jennifer Bentson, 12" x 9", Watercolor

Painted under the oaks at Nuncio's Nursery.

ARC ANGEL

My career as a vocational consultant started as a series of unplanned events. Despite the resumé blasts after I graduated from college, my career direction began when I took an extension class. The student sitting next to me asked if I wanted to interview with her company in a new field, private vocational rehabilitation. I did, and stayed with this career until the benefit ceased.

Basically I was contracted by various insurance companies, self-insureds, and TPA's to provide career services to the disabled.

One of the people I worked with was a CPA who had had a double lung transplant. He had been out of work for a couple of years and so I helped him with his resume and job search. He quickly went back to work and before no time, was able to sustain a full time schedule. This was such a successful case, that the insurance company created a video of my client and me at his new job. After the case was closed we met a couple of times for lunch and I met his wife.

Sadly, the rejection drugs and complications claimed my client's life after about 10 years. Coincidentially, I had lost my husband the year before. When I called to offer my condolences to his wife, we decided to meet. Since then we have become great friends. This angle is from her garden on the border of Pasadena. The oak in the background forms an arch or arc. And since she and I both have angels in heaven, I thought this painting was a great tribute.

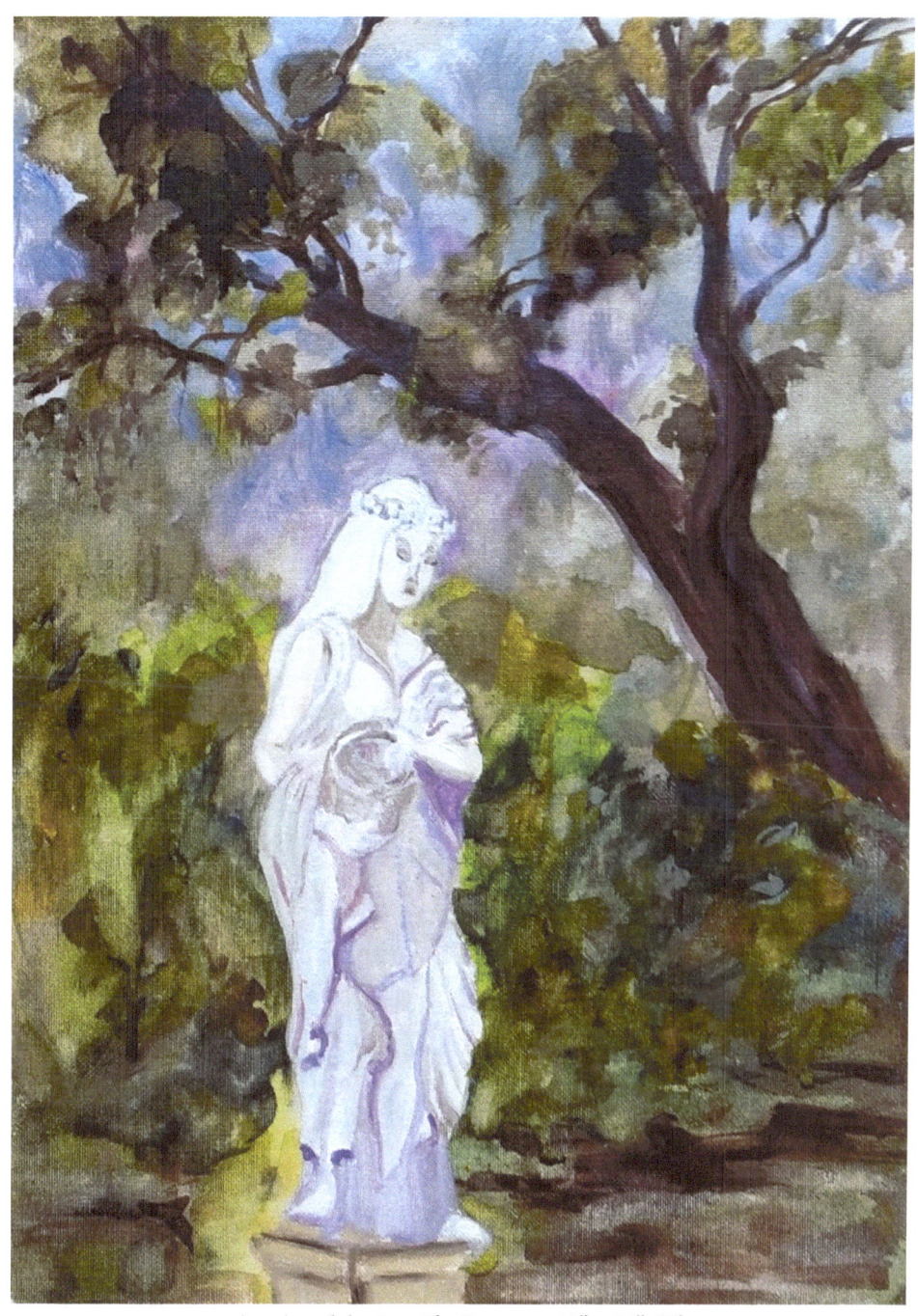

Arc Angel, by Jennifer Bentson, 12" x 16", Oil

Painted in my Studio

CHELTEN WAY OAKS

Chelten Way, located in South Pasadena, is home to a street with oak trees growing out of the pavement. At one time the city council wanted to cut down the oak trees and pave over them. The community banded together and saved these trees. The newspaper article read, "Ax the city council, not the oaks." Today the street is closed off at one end and the oaks are thriving.

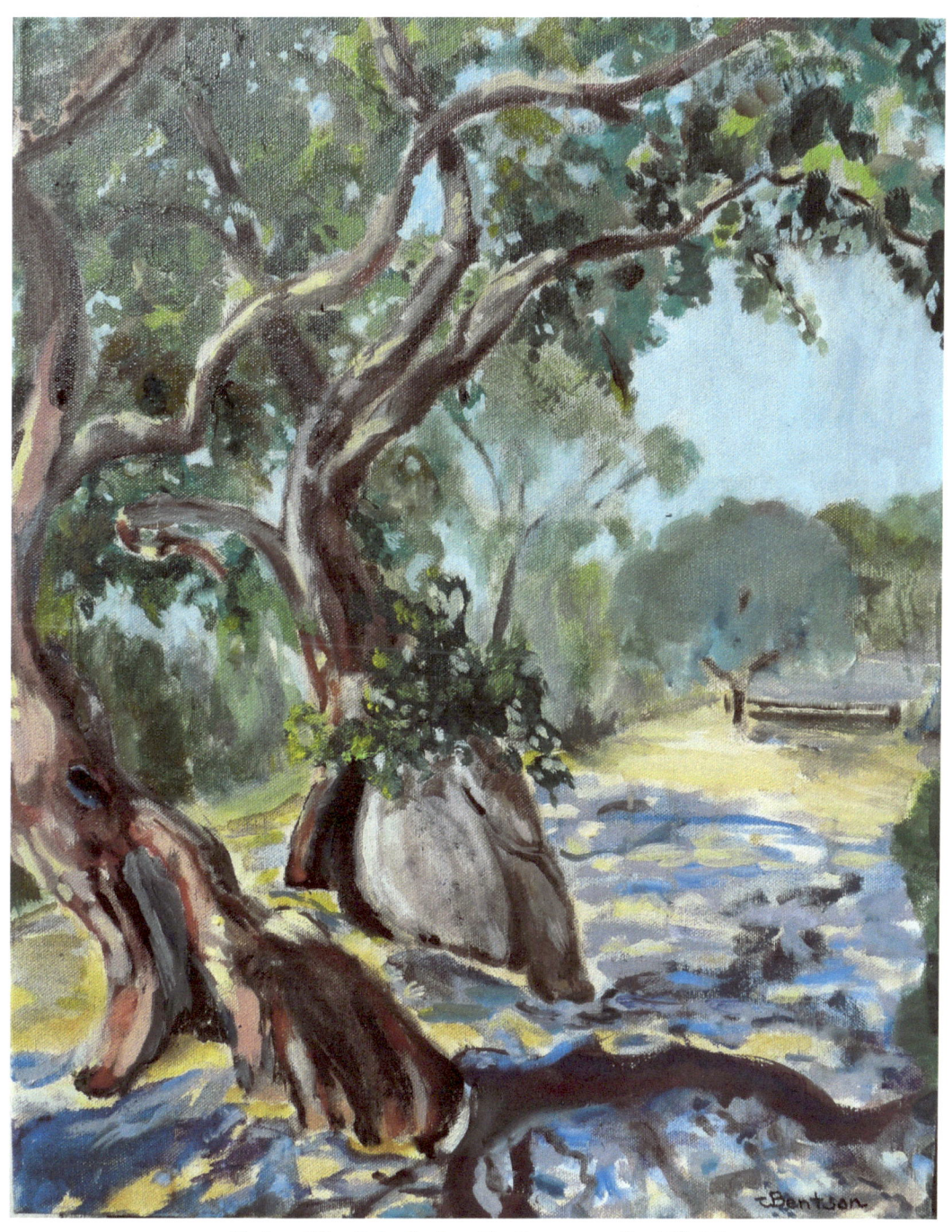

Chelten Way Oaks, by Jennifer Bentson, 16" x 20", Oil

Painted in Studio

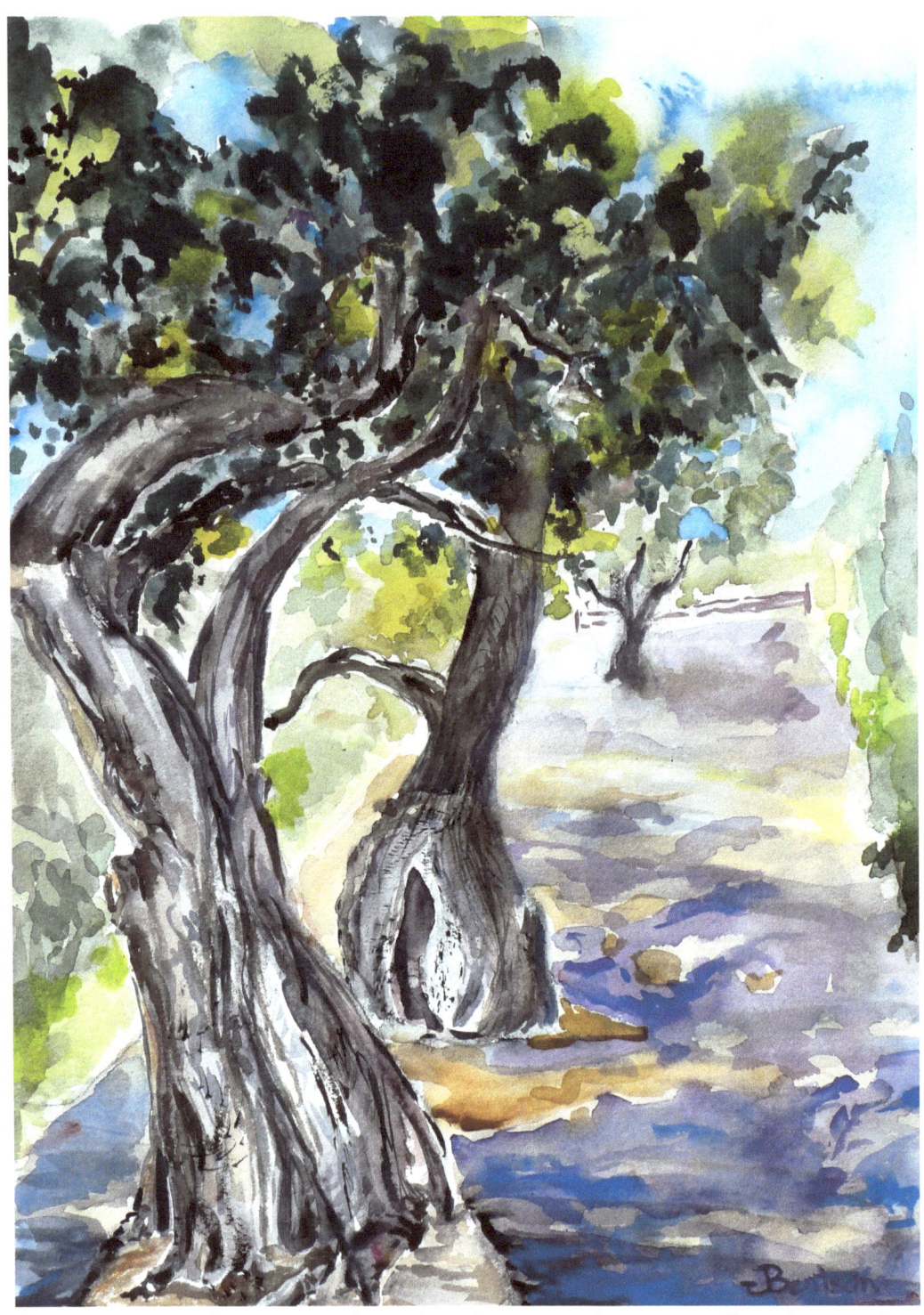

Chelten Way, Ax the City Council, Not the Oaks, By Jennifer Bentson, 9" x 12", Watercolor

Painted on Location

Oak Locations

Page i, Largest Engelmann Oak in the USA, Big List of Trees, USA, California Avenue - private esidence
Page 1, Oaks Looking Skyward, Descanso Gardens, 1418 Descanso Drive, Flintridge, La Canada, 91011
Page 2, Oaks, Descanso Gardens, 1418 Descanso Drive, Flintridge, La Canada, 91011
Page 3, Limbs and Legs, Lower Arroyo Seco, Pasadena
Page 4, Arroyo Oak, Lower Arroyo Seco, Pasadena, CA 91105
Page 5, Hahamongna Oak Grove, 101 Foothill, La Canada, 91011
Page 8 and 9, Jennifer Bentson's home, Chevy Chase Canyon, Glendale 91206
Page 10, Engelmann Oak Path to City Hall, East Holly Street, between Marengo and Garfield, Pasadena, 91101
Page 11, Memorial Park, Corner of Walnut and Raymond, Pasadena, 91101
Page 15, Frank's Family Tree, Private Residence, Hastings Ranch, Pasadena
Page 17, Mama Oak, Eaton Canyon Nature Center, 1750 N Altadena Dr, Pasadena 91107
Page 18, A Walk in the Forest, Eaton Canyon Nature Center, 1750 N Altadena Dr, Pasadena 91107
Page 20, Reflecting Under an Oak, Eaton Canyon Nature Center, 1750 N Altadena Dr, Pasadena 91107
Page 21, Eaton Canyon Path, Eaton Canyon Nature Center, 1750 N Altadena Dr, Pasadena 91107
Page 24, Sidestreet Oak, Corner of Fair Oaks and Orange Grove near Church's, Pasadena, 91103
Page 27, Open for Prayer, Westminster Presbyterian Church, 1757 N Lake Ave, Pasadena, CA 91104
Page 29, Busch Garden Oaks, Lower Arroyo Canyon, Pasadena, CA 91105
Page 31, A Tale of Two Trees, Orange Grove Blvd. Between California and Columbia, Pasadena, CA
Page 32, La Loma Street Bridge, National Historical Register, La Loma Ave at Arroyo Seco, Pasadena, CA 91105
Page 33, La Loma Street Bridge, National Historical Register, La Loma Ave at Arroyo Seco, Pasadena, CA 91105
Page 35, On the Edge of the Worldwide Church of God, Green Street near Orange Grove, Pasadena 91105
Page 37, On the Edge of the Worldwide Church of God, Green Street near Orange Grove, Pasadena 91105
Page 40, Caltech Engelmann Oak, Caltech, 1200 East California, Pasadena, CA 91125
Page 41, Throop Hall, Caltech, 1200 East California, Pasadena, CA 91125
Page 42, View of the Great Oak from Arch, Caltech, 1200 East California, Pasadena, CA 91125
Page 43, Hunt Plot Plan, Caltech, 1200 East California, Pasadena, CA 91125
Page 44, Caltech Hot, Caltech, 1200 East California, Pasadena, CA 91125
Page 45, Photo Caltech Archives, Caltech, 1200 East California, Pasadena, CA 91125
Page 46, Caltech Engelmann Oak in Full Canopy, Caltech, 1200 East California, Pasadena, CA 91125
Page 47, Caltech Engelmann Oak, Caltech, 1200 East California, Pasadena, CA 91125
Page 49, Engelmann Oak at Caltech and Roses, Caltech, 1200 East California, Pasadena, CA 91125
Page 51, Huntington's Mausoleum Shaded by Engelmann Oak, The Huntington Library, Art Collections, and Botanical Gardens, 1151 Oxford Road, San Marino, CA 91108
Page 53, Huntington Garden's Canary Isle Oak, The Huntington Library, Art Collections, and Botanical Gardens, 1151 Oxford Road, San Marino, CA 91108
Page 54, Lombardy Oak, Lombardy and San Marino St., Pasadena, CA 91108
Page 55, Lombardy Street Oak, Lombardy and San Marino St., Pasadena, CA 91108
Page 57, Largest Engelmann Oak in the USA, Private Residence, California Avenue, Pasadena
Page 61, Charlie Parker Slept Here, Zorthian Ranch, 3990 Fair Oaks Ave., Altadena, CA 91001
Page 63, Under the Oaks at Nuncio's Nursery, 3555 Chaney Trail, Altadena, CA 91001
Page 65, Arc Angel, Private Residence, Altadena, CA 91001
Page 67, Chelten Way Oaks, Chelten Way and Monterey Ave, South Pasadena, CA 91030
Page 68, Chelten Way, Ax the City Council Not the Oaks, Chelten Way & Monterey Ave, South Pasadena, CA 91030

The Tanka Tour of the Caltech Campus is being created by Caltech community and local poets. We love Caltech's beauty and inspiration. Here is a sampling from our second stop on the tour, The 400 Year Old Tree:

Kath Abela Wilson

centuries flow
through her heartwood
I wish for a long life
of outstretched arms
and silent witness

published Sept 2012 One Hundred Gourds

Joan E. Stern

arms spread far and wide
needing strong tensile support
four centuries pass
oak acknowledges harsh wounds
history repeats itself

Taura Scott

ancient oak propped up
so tired
your boughs
all that you have left
we are not so different

Erika Wilk

the old oak's limbs
resemble acrobats
youthful
on each others' shoulders
in gusts of wind some tumble

Kath Abela Wilson

400 years
and then one windstorm
whitewashed at the breaks
I think of the story
of my old love

Mira Mataric

a sage, you graceful tree
arms stretched
like in a fertile mother
silently teaching
perseverance

Joan E. Stern

rancho giant
granted by Lincoln
adapts or dies
disease and lightning strikes
temporary setbacks

Susan Rogers

oh wise oak
can you tell me about the air
400 years ago
I breathe into your gnarled trunk
into your richly storied bark and listen

Sharon Hawley

a raven saw you in your youth
a Chumash brushed your branch
John Muir might have befriended you
but it took an oak doctor
to shore up your old age

Peggy Castro

beneath a canopy of leaves
the weight of 400 years
supported by loving buttresses
I feel the pain
of your aching limbs

Lisa Tibbs

standing your ground
pondering
how many great brains
have sat beneath your boughs
expanding knowledge

Claire Everett

a gentle rain
as I climb higher
russet and gold
voices of my ancestors
shaken loose from the tree

Kath Abela Wilson

under centuries old oak
after the windstorm
a sudden scent of roses
scrap of scribbled verse
in the earth by her roots

Amanda Dcosta

nestled in the
aged branches of this
wooden heart
chirping of new life
resonates

The Tour Poets will be accompanied on flute by Kathabela's husband mathematics professor Rick Wilson, sometimes other friend musicians on quiet guitar, ukukele or mandolin.

Thanks to Barbara Ellis and the Caltech Women's Club for appreciating our tour *created by Kathabela Wilson* kaw@oldflutes.com

(Editor note: K. Wilson spells her name Kath Abela for poetry, and Kathabela for all else.)

Take the Tanka Tour
by Kathabela Wilson

As many of you know, I host the Caltech Red Door Poets group. A special subgroup of these poets write a type of short poetry, called "tanka," which is a five-line lyrical Japanese form. It is free, emotionally expressive, and musical in its quality. This group, led by me, has created a "Tanka Tour of the Caltech Campus." We have so far written short poems at eight different locations: the Red Door Café, the 400-year-old oak tree, the turtle pond, Dabney Gardens, the lily pond by Ramo, the entrance to the Humanities library ("The Enchanted Library"), the grove of silk floss trees, and the Olive Walk.

Starting in November, the poets will give a sampling of the tour at one or more locations each week. Every Wednesday at 1:00 pm, the Tour will start at the outside tables of the Red Door Café. After a short introduction, we will move on to the next sites at 1:15 pm, and finish at 1:35 pm. Look for my Flowery Hat to locate the group at the Red Door Café.

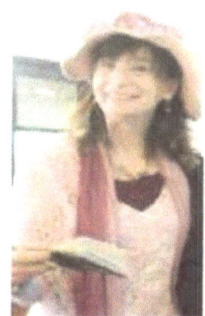

**The Tanka Tour of the Caltech Campus
by
Tanka Poets on Site**
Red Door Poets
The Caltech Poetry Club

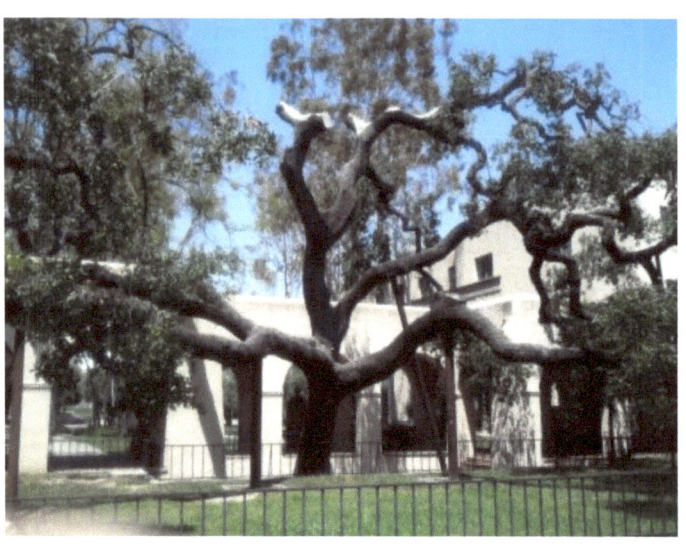

**Second Stop:
The 400 Year Old Tree**
Drawing by Janet Olenik

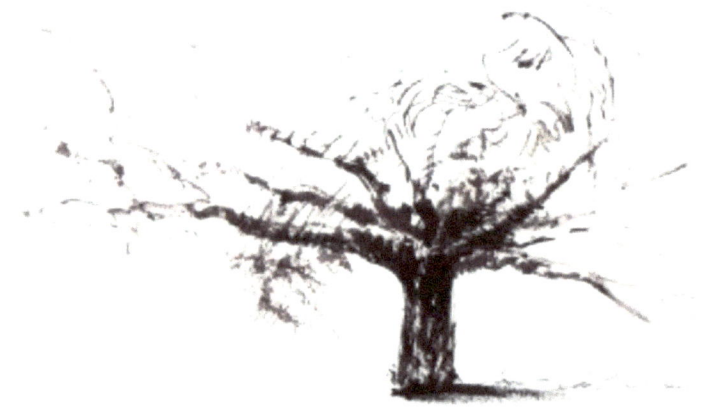

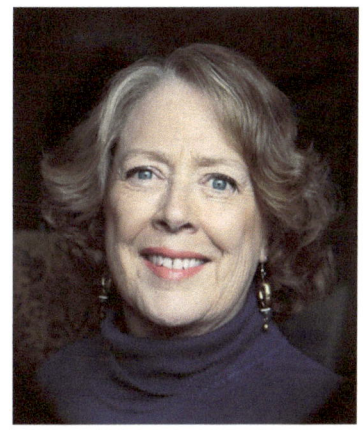

Jennifer Bentson, Artist

Bio

<u>Mediums:</u>
Watercolor
Oil,
Acrylic
Sketch - Charcoal, Pencil, and Pastel,
Print,
Chinese Brush Painting.

<u>Commissions</u>
California Technical Institute, Engelmann Oak, 2011
State of California, Air Resources Board, 2004

<u>Publications</u>
Six Visions, Wapshott Press
Storylandia, Wapshott Press, Cover 2013
Erotique, Wapshott Press Cover 2013, 2014
Chevy Chase Garden Cub, Member's Directory, 2012
California State Garden Clubs, California Poppy, 2012
Current Correspondent for Art Quench Magazine, www.artquenchmagazine.com
- "Say it with Costume" at FIDM, Art Quench Magazine Online, April 19, 2016
- "LA Art Show Stretches Your Imagination", Art Quench Magazine Online, Feb. 23, 2016
- "Hi From Kauai", Art Quench Magazine Online, April 30, 2015
- "No SCUBA Gear Required" Long Beach Aquarium of the Pacific, Art Quench Magazine Online, January 30, 2015
- "Art Auction In Action " Bonham's supports APLA, Art Quench Magazine Online, June 20, 2015
- "Hunting Jackalope Arts in Pasadena Ca." Art Quench Magazine Online, May 8, 2016

- "Odd Night on the Sod at the Autry Museum" Art Quench Magazine Online, June 8, 2015
- Jennifer Bentson, featured artist, AQM Creative Masters, Volume One
- "Art, Cross Polination of China and California, AQM, Vol. Two, pgs 72-78
- Jennifer Bentson, featured artist, AQM International Artist, pgs 22-23
- "Vissi d'Arte" Jennifer Bentson visits Italy and France, AQM, Vol. Three
- Pasadena Oaks, 75 Page Book of Art and Stories, due to be printed June, 2016

Exhibits:
Chevy Chase Country Club – Solo Show 2009
Highland Taffy Art Assn., Summer Art Shows 2009, 2010, 2011, 2015
Brand Library, Glendale, CA , 2010
Modern Art Gallery, Los Angeles, CA, March, 2010
Descanso Gardens Art Gallery, La Canada, CA 1995, 1996
Montrose Art Walk – 2010, 2011
Bluebird House Art Gallery, Juried 2010
California State Air Resources Board, 2000-2010
The Advocate Gallery, Juried 12-6- 2010 to 1-20-2011, Hollywood, CA
Segil Fine Art Gallery, Juried 2011, 2012
North Hollywood Performing Arts Center, Juried 2011
Gallery 800, Juried 2011, Juried 2012 winner of Windsor Newton Watercolor Award. Juried 2013
Bonham and Butterfields 2011, APLA Juried 2012. 2013, 2014, 2015
California Institute of Technology, Permanent Collection 2011- present
Theodore Payne Foundation, Juried 2012
GAA – Silverlake Citibank Gallery - Group Show 2012
White's Gallery 2012 – (Two Shows) Fall Salon and October Show
Huntington Gardens and Library – Juried Show, 2012
La Canada Library – 2013 April Show
Anzoh Gallery – GAA – June 2013 Show
Burbank Creative Arts Gallery – July 2013 – Winner 2nd place, Watercolor
Glendale Youth Alliance, Juried Show, Nov. 2013
Valley Visions, Juried Show, June 2014, Winner "First Place Watercolor" Also chosen for cover of the catalog
Thousand Oaks Gallery, "California Oaks as Art" 27 pieces with interpretative information Also chosen for cover of the catalog
Art Director's Guild, Gallery 800, Figurative Art Show
Theodore Payne Foundation, Juried Art Show, 2014
GAA, Juried Show, October 2014, Winner "Honorable Mention" Sculpture
Lark Gallery, Brea Show, 2014-5
Aquarium of the Pacific, 2014, One of 20 artists juried into show.
Aquarium of the Pacific, 2015, One of 23 artists juried into show
Glendale Youth Authority, Juried Show, 2015
Far Niente, Curator, Oct. 2014 to March 2015, over 40 pieces of art hung on a monthly rotating schedule.
Glendale Area Loves Art, Curator, Spring Show, 2015
White's Gallery, GAA Spring Show, Juried, Winner "Honorable Mention" Figurative 2015

Blick Art Store Gallery, Pasadena, May, 2015
Civitella d'Agliano Italy, July 2015
Thousand Oaks Art Gallery, August 2015, winner "Honorable Mention" for Oak Trees.
San Fernando Valley Culture and Arts Center, October, winner "Honorable Mention" 2015
DIGGS Gallery, Montrose, CA 2015-6
The Tiny Gallery, Nuremberg, Germany, 2016
The City of Pasadena Main Library, May 2-31, 2106, Featured Artist for 6 cases of 30 pieces of artwork.
Caltech, Solo Exhibition, June 11, 2016 "Pasadena Oaks", Paintings and Book Reception

Public Art
2015, Utility Box, City of Glendale, corner of Boynton and Chevy Chase.
2016, Utility Box, City of LA, Sunland/Tujunga, corner of Foothill and Wentworth, YouTube, "Artists, Jennifer Bentson and Gary McBride"

Exhibitions Produced
2013, Love of Art, Gallery 800, 50 participants, 95 pieces of art, SFVAC
2013 Masters of SFVAC Exhibition, CSUN Gallery, May, 2012, 22 artists, 34 pieces of art
2013 Small is Beautiful, White's Gallery, 31 artists, 76 pieces of art
2014 Theodore Payne Foundation, Paint Out and Subsequent Gallery Show, 22 artists
2014 Thousand Oaks Gallery, open call, 43 artists, 87 pieces
2014 Thousand Oaks Gallery, 6 Visions Show, 6 artists, 95 pieces of art, published catalog created featuring the artists.
2014-5 Far Niente Restaurant, Glendale, CA, negotiated management of the walls of art for the restaurant. New show every two months, since October, 2014
2015 GALA, Glendale Area Loves Art, As GAA President, I curated and organized this show in a short period of time.

Presentations on "California Oaks as Art" Project
Chevy Chase Garden Club – 2012
Los Angeles County Arboretum – 2013
Delegate to China representing SFVAC – September 2014

Education:
BA Education, University of Arizona
MS Post Graduate Coursework in Educational Psychology

Professional Art Courses
Chinese Brush Painting, Xiamen University, Gulangyu Island, China
Figure and Portrait Painting – Animation Guild, Burbank, CA
Ceramics – La Canada Adult School – 2 sessions
Watercolor Painting – Glendale Adult School (7 sessions) and Monrovia Adult School (1 session)
Oil Painting – Glendale Adult School (3 sessions)
Figure Drawing – Glendale Adult School (3 sessions)

Perspective, Animation Guild, Burbank, CA

Leadership Roles
President, Glendale Art Association, 2015
President, San Fernando Valley Art Club (2013-4)
American Society for Training and Development – Member of Board of Directors (Workshop Director) (Career Services Director) - 3 years
Treasurer for the Glendale Symphony Orchestra Association – 2 years
Workshop Developer – Youth Rights at Work – presented to Glendale Explorers with EEO

Artist Tour/Exchange
2013, Invitation to Lin Zaifu, Chinese Brush Artist, Xiamen, China, to USA for presentation to SFVAC.
2014, Organized and led group of artists from SFVAC to China. Painted with Chinese artists in Xiamen and Guilin, China
2015 Selected to attend ArtLab in Italy and paint with many Italian Artists for 2 weeks. An exhibition of our artwork produced during the two weeks was held in an ancient castle.
2015, Invitation to Yongwei Yang, University of Guilin Professor of Art for presentation to
SFVAC and Exhibition, Hosted Yongwei Yong and his wife

Employment History:
2015 - present
    Art Quench Magazine, Correspondent
2006-present
    Artist, Self Employed, www.jenniferbentson.com
2006-present
    Property Manager
1987- 2009
    Vocational Consultant, Network Career Counseling
    Self Employed, owner of www.networkcareer.com
1978-1987
    Vocational Consultant, Workworld, Inc.
1977-1978
    Director, Glendale Women's Center
1974-1977
    Classroom teacher, LAUSD

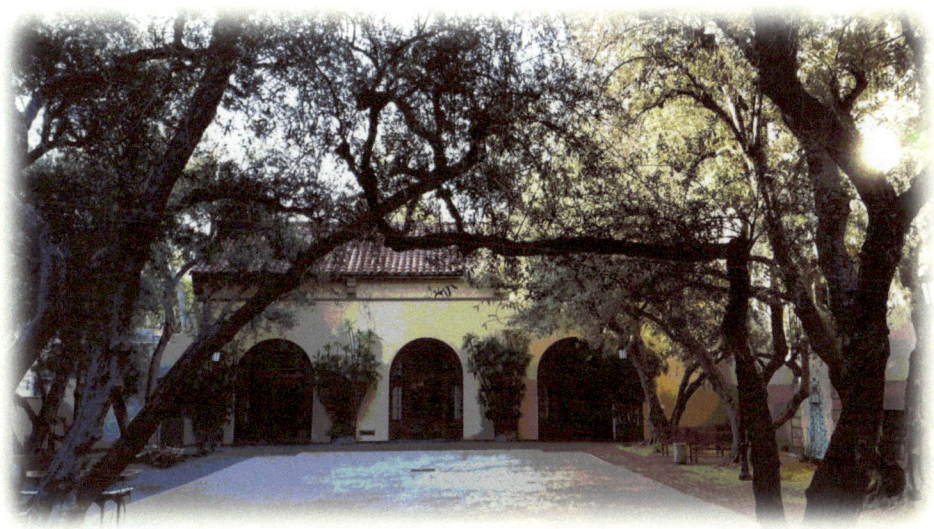

Please join us for an

Oak Tree Tea

Featuring an Exhibition of Art and the stories of the significant oak trees of Pasadena as created by Jennifer Bentson, Artist.

We will honor the 400-Year Old Engelmann Oak at Caltech as well as other oak trees that have shaped Pasadena and the surrounding community. Each oak tree has a story to tell and through Jennifer's paintings and the people she has met on this journey the community of Pasadena and their significant oaks will be enjoyed.
The Caltech Poets on Site, led by Kathabela Wilson, will read selections about the Great Oak of Caltech.

June 11, 2016, Saturday
From 3PM to 6PM

At Dabney Hall, California Institute of Technology
Pasadena, CA

Light refreshments will be served.
This event is free. RSVP: bentson9@gmail.com
Hosted by Caltech
and

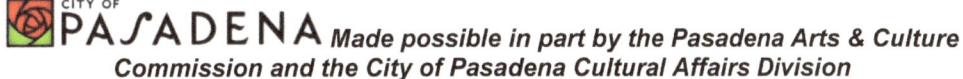 *Made possible in part by the Pasadena Arts & Culture Commission and the City of Pasadena Cultural Affairs Division*

www.ingramcontent.com/pod-product-compliance
Lightning Source LLC
Chambersburg PA
CBHW051156220526
45473CB00003B/796